100 Case Histories fo

100 Case Histories for the MRCP

David J. Spalton MRCP, FRCS
Consultant Ophthalmologist,
Charing Cross Hospital, London

Peter S. Sever PhD, FRCP
Professor of Clinical Pharmacology,
St. Mary's Hospital, London

Peter Dorrington Ward MRCP
Senior Registrar in Medicine,
Charing Cross Hospital, London

Second Edition revised by

John Armitstead MRCP
Medical Registrar,
St. Mary's Hospital, London

Michael Greenstone MRCP
Medical Registrar,
St. Mary's Hospital, London

Foreword by
E.E. Keal MD, FRCP
Consultant Physician and Dean,
Brompton Hospital, London

SECOND EDITION

CHURCHILL LIVINGSTONE
EDINBURGH LONDON MELBOURNE AND NEW YORK 1982

CHURCHILL LIVINGSTONE
Medical Division of Longman Group Limited

Distributed in the United States of America by Churchill
Livingstone Inc., 1560 Broadway, New York, N.Y.
10036, and by associated companies, branches and
representatives throughout the world.

First edition 1976
Second edition 1982
  Reprinted 1985

ISBN 0 443 02140 6

British Library Cataloguing in Publication Data
Spalton, David J.
   100 case histories for the MRCP. — 2nd ed.
   1. Diseases — Case studies
   I. Title   II. Sever, Peter S.
   III. Dorrington Ward, Peter
   616'.09   RC66

Library of Congress Catalog Card Number 81-70331

Produced by Longman Singapore Publishers Pte Ltd.
Printed in Singapore.

Foreword

It is sad and frustrating to have a meticulous history and physical examination presented by a houseman or candidate and to realise at the end that the trees are lost in the wood and that there is no awareness of the diagnostic problem, its logical investigation and its management in the best interests of the patient. This is not an uncommon situation that reflects badly on both teacher and student.

The authors have undertaken the formidable task of trying to remedy this state of affairs, mainly for the benefit of Membership candidates but, *ipso facto*, for the better practice of medicine. The book is not a textbook of medicine, a collection of lecture notes or an aid to multiple choice questions. There are plenty of these. Instead it gives the relevant findings in a hundred authentic patients presenting to acute medical wards and invites the reader to exercise his own clinical judgement before turning to the discussion which highlights the salient features of each case. Used in this way the book will be a valuable aid to prospective candidates.

London, 1982   E.E.K.

Preface

Since this book was published in 1976, it has become established as part of the revision for the majority of candidates taking the MRCP examination in the U.K. and has also acquired a large following amongst those taking similar examinations overseas.

With the preparation of this new edition, we have taken note of the major changes in the techniques of investigation of disease that have occurred during the past five years. Consequently, each case history has been re-written and scrutinised by experts in the field. Many new cases have been added and the paediatric and psychiatric cases have been removed, reflecting the changes in the MRCP examination. The brunt of this work has fallen on our friends, John Armitstead and Michael Greenstone, but we would also like to thank other colleagues too numerous to mention who have given freely of their time and expertise. We hope this new edition will be scientifically accurate and thought-provoking. We believe also that students not committed to the MRCP examination will find the cases enjoyable and stimulating.

London, 1982

D.J.S.
P.S.S.
P.D.W.

Introduction

The MRCP has a reputation of being a difficult examination but, provided it is approached sensibly, one can save an enormous amount of time and effort by concentrating on the subjects that lend themselves to this form of examination. A brief review of former papers shows that some topics appear more often than others and it is vital that any candidate has complete competence in these subjects before extending his knowledge to minutiae which can be largely irrelevant in the success or failure at the examination. Examiners tell us that the examination is designed to test clinical wisdom, insight and practicality rather than an encyclopaedic knowledge. Many people fail themselves by simple ignorance of basic facts or by saying or doing stupid things that indicate a lack of understanding of elementary principles and common sense. The first precept, therefore, is to have a sound basic knowledge and to be able to apply this to clinical problems.

Our book provides a series of cases for revision for Part II of the examination. These hundred cases are all based on actual patients and are of a similar standard and format to those that one expects to meet in the examination. It is the intention that the problems will assess one's knowledge of a subject and indicate deficiencies or areas that need further attention. They are all 'grey' cases and as such are open to different interpretations. In the synopsis of each case those answers that we consider would be most acceptable are printed in capital letters. Obviously some answers are more important than others and would gain more marks. However, these cases are 'grey' and you may arrive at different conclusions but, if so, you must be able to substantiate your reasoning carefully.

Whilst these case histories are directed to the papers, they represent the type of patient that you might expect to face in the clinical section. This is the part of the examination where skill and technique are paramount and in which there is no substitute for practice and experience.

Case 1

A 46-year-old petrol pump attendant was admitted as an emergency. He had smoked 20 cigarettes a day for many years, but apart from several episodes of acute bronchitis had always been well. Ten days previously he had become ill with generalised weakness, anorexia and a dry cough. His own doctor had prescribed tetracycline and he had started to feel a little better despite a worsening cough and increasing exertional dyspnoea. Two days before admission, he had developed diarrhoea and on the day of admission he became confused.

On admission to hospital he was cyanosed, febrile (38.5°C) and disorientated. Blood pressure was 125/78 mmHg, pulse 110 beats per minute, regular, with no evidence of heart failure. The breath sounds were diminished at both bases with widespread inspiratory crackles to the midzone and bronchial breathing at the right base. There were no abnormalities of the abdomen or focal neurological signs.

Investigations: Hb 12.9 g/dl (12.9 g%), WBC 9.0 × 10⁹/l (9000/mm³) (93% polymorphs, 6% lymphocytes, 1% eosinophils). Platelets 120 × 10⁹/l (120 000/mm³), ESR 86 mm/hr. Sodium 129 mmol/l (129 mEq/l), potassium 4.3 mmol/l (4.3 mEq/l), urea 5.9 mmol/l (35 mg%), blood sugar 6.8 mmol/l (122 mg%). Liver function tests: albumin 28 g/l (2.8 g%), aspartate transaminase 60 U/l; bilirubin 12 μmol/l (0.70 mg%), HBD 190 U/l, alkaline phosphatase 145 U/l. Chest X-ray showed widespread shadowing in both lung fields with relative sparing of the apices and consolidation at the right base. Blood gases – pO₂ 7.9 kPa (59 mmHg), pCO₂ 4.7 kPa (35 mmHg), pH 7.39. Electrocardiogram showed a sinus tachycardia.

He was thought to have widespread bronchopneumonia and was started on intravenous ampicillin and flucloxacillin. The next day his condition markedly deteriorated with increasing dyspnoea, confusion and cyanosis. ECG showed no change and blood gases showed at pO₂ of 6.4 kPa (48 mm Hg), pCO₂ 4.8 kPa (36 mmHg), and pH 7.36. Repeat chest X-ray showed increased shadowing in both lung fields and early involvement of the right apex.

1. What is the diagnosis?
2. How would you confirm this and give four other useful investigations?

Atypical pneumonia eg Legionella.
Alb

The patient has an acute severe pneumonia with a prodromal illness that has failed to respond to several antibiotics. This raises the possibility of an atypical infective agent. His sudden deterioration could have been caused by a worsening of his pneumonia, a pneumothorax, massive pulmonary collapse or even a pulmonary embolus. A repeat chest X-ray and blood gas would help to distinguish these. Further attempts to isolate the organism would be made and include BLOOD CULTURES and BRONCHOSCOPY or TRANSTRACHEAL ASPIRATION OF SPUTUM in the event of a non-productive cough. SERUM FOR VIRAL ANTIBODIES could include the commoner viruses or 'atypical' agents including mycoplasma pneumoniae and psittacosis.

This man has not responded to tetracycline which makes a diagnosis of mycoplasma and psittacosis unlikely. He does have a relatively low white cell count with lymphopenia, midly abnormal LFTs, diarrhoea and a degree of confusion out of proportion to his hypoxia or hyponatraemia. These features are all typical of LEGIONNAIRE'S DISEASE, and the diagnosis is confirmed by the development of ANTIBODIES TO LEGIONELLA PNEUMOPHILIA during the course of the illness. Because seroconversion takes up to two weeks, the diagnosis must be made clinically if effective treatment is to be started early. Other features of the disease include a relative bradycardia, pleurisy, hypophosphataemia, abnormal liver function tests, gastrointestinal symptoms, confusion, proteinuria and a mild coagulopathy. This patient has low platelets and a CLOTTING SCREEN including fibrin degradation products should be performed. Culture of the organism is difficult.

Treatment is usually with erythromycin and/or rifampicin. A smaller percentage of patients respond to tetracycline but this can no longer be regarded as the treatment of choice.

2

Case 2

A 47-year-old housewife was referred to the dermatology clinic with a complaint of generalised pruritis for one year. This had started insidiously but had recently become troublesome, keeping her awake at night. She otherwise felt well, with a good appetite and steady weight, but did admit to a dry mouth. She did not smoke, drank occasionally and was on no medication. No other members of her family had experienced itching.

On examination, she looked well and was not anaemic, jaundiced, cyanosed or clubbed. There was no lymphadenopathy. There were scattered scratch marks, but no other skin lesions were seen. Cardiovascular and respiratory systems normal. In her abdomen, the liver was palpable two finger breadths below the costal margin. No other masses were palpable and the spleen could not be felt. Urinalysis was negative.

Investigations: Hb 13.7 g/dl (13.7 g%) (normal film), WBC 5.8 × 10^9/l (5800/mm^3), sodium 137 mmol/l (137 mEq/l), potassium 4.2 mmol/l (4.2 mEq/l), bicarbonate 24 mmol/l (24 mEq/l), urea 5.2 mmol/l (31 mg%), aspartate transaminase 36 U/l, bilirubin 12 μmol/l (0.70 mg%), protein 64 g/l (6.4 g%), with albumin 37 g/l (3.7 g%), alkaline phosphatase 470 U/l, calcium 2.35 mmol/l (9.4 mg%), phosphate 0.80 mmol/l (2.5 mg%), fasting glucose 4.5 mmol/l (80 mg%), thyroxine 125 mmol/l (9.7 μg%), free thyroxine index 135. Chest X-ray normal.

1. What is the most likely diagnosis?
2. How would you confirm this?
3. What treatment would you give?

This lady raises the differential diagnosis of pruritis. There is no evidence of specific skin disease and so a systemic cause is suggested. Malignancy can present this way, but her history is long and there is no evidence on examination. Similarly a reticulosis or myeloproliferative disorder is unlikely. Her investigations exclude uraemia, diabetes, myxoedema, hyperthyroidism or jaundice as causes.

Her one abnormal investigation is the raised alkaline phosphatase and this suggests the diagnosis of PRIMARY BILIARY CIRRHOSIS. Approximately 50% of patients with this disease present with pruritis and most sufferers develop this symptom at some stage during their disease. The pruritis may be present for some years before jaundice develops.

Although the diagnosis is also suggested by finding a high level of serum IgM or a positive anti-mitochondrial antibody titre, confirmation is obtained by LIVER BIOPSY. In the early stages bile duct damage is shown by swelling and proliferation of epithelial cells and the ducts are surrounded by a dense inflammatory infiltrate of lymphocytes and plasma cells with epithelioid cells and a few eosinophils. Granulomata may be seen. Later the lesions become more widespread, although less specific, and fibrosis occurs ending in cirrhosis.

Treatment of primary biliary cirrhosis is unsatisfactory. In view of the possible immunological aetiology, immuno-suppressive therapy has been tried. Corticosteroids have not been tested in a controlled trial as there is no convincing evidence that they might alter the progression of the disease and there are fears that they might accelerate the development of osteoporosis. Azathioprine is being evaluated in a controlled trial and although results suggest that it might be of benefit, these have not yet attained statistical significance. Another drug that is used in some centres is Penicillamine, again with no definite evidence of benefit. Pruritis can be treated with cholestyramine, and there is some evidence that phototherapy may be of benefit. Supplements of fat-soluble vitamins and calcium should be given.

Case 3

A 25-year-old Dutch woman presented to medical out-patients with a three-month history of increasing thirst and polyuria. During this time she had put on two stone in weight. Four months previously she had had a mastoid operation and subsequently developed irregular periods.

There was no other past medical history of note and in her family history one sister had been treated for thyrotoxicosis.
Examination was entirely normal.

Investigations showed: urea and electrolytes, calcium and phosphate, glucose tolerance test – all normal. Mid-stream urine showed no growth.

1. Give two possible diagnoses.
2. Describe the test which would distinguish between these. Are any hazards associated with this test?
3. Give three further investigations.

This young woman either has DIABETES INSIPIDUS or COMPULSIVE WATER DRINKING. Her normal glucose tolerance test excludes diabetes mellitus and her normal calcium and potassium rule out the common causes of renal tubular damage which may give rise to polyuria.

A formal fluid deprivation measuring urine and serum osmolalities, with regular weighing in hospital under observation, will show if she can concentrate her urine. The test can be hazardous due to excessive loss of fluid and should be terminated if the subject loses more than 3% of initial body weight. An injection of synthetic antidiuretic hormone (DDAVP) should be given at the end of the test to see if exogenous ADH causes urine concentration, as would be expected in pituitary causes of diabetes insipidus where there is lack of antidiuretic hormone.

This woman failed to concentrate her urine during fluid deprivation, but did so after injection of DDAVP, proving pituitary diabetes insipidus. Though in the majority of patients no underlying cause can be found, it is important to exclude a pituitary tumour. She should have a pituitary X-ray, and COMPUTERISED AXIAL TOMOGRAPHY (CT SCAN), as well as having her visual fields assessed. Head trauma may precede the development of diabetes insipidus, though there is no history of this here. Rarer causes include granulomatous disease and local infections, including basal meningitis. Any relationship of her developing diabetes insipidus with her previous mastoid surgery remains only speculative.

Case 4

A 74-year-old widow is referred to the Out-Patient Department for investigation. She had been found to be hypertensive four months previously and had been managed by her general practitioner with a diuretic and a small dose of propranolol. Because of postural hypotension, this treatment had been stopped one month later and her GP had encouraged her to lose weight while carefully observing her blood pressure. Two months before admission she had been found wandering around the house in a confused state by her daughter with whom she lived. By the next morning she was better and her doctor ascribed the attack to transient cerebral ischaemia. At this time, her blood pressure was noted to be 180/105 and her doctor restarted her on bendrofluazide 5 mg daily. She was well for several weeks, but her daughter noticed her becoming forgetful and losing interest in her grandchildren, on one occasion forgetting their names. There were no other symptoms apart from her longstanding constipation for which she took a proprietary laxative.

On examination, she was moderately obese. Her blood pressure was 175/105 mmHg sitting and standing; pulse rate was 70 per minute and regular. Heart sounds were normal and there was no evidence of cardiac failure. Her fundi showed grade II hypertensive changes. The chest and abdomen were normal. Examination of her central nervous system revealed that she was rather depressed, but answered questions slowly but accurately. Her reflexes were bilaterally brisk, but there was no focal weakness. Vibration sense was diminished at both ankles, but other sensory modalities were normal. Both plantar responses were extensor.

Investigations showed: Hb 12.0 g/dl (12.0 g%), WBC 4.8 × 10^9/l (4800/mm^3), ESR 29 mm/h, MCV 86 fl (86 μ^3). Sodium 133 mmol/l (133 mEq/l), potassium 3.8 mmol/l (3.8 mEq/l), urea 7.8 mmol/l (47 mg%). Random blood sugar 8.7 mmol/l (157 mg%), calcium 2.34 mmol/l (9.36 mEq/l). Chest and skull X-rays were normal. Serum calcium was normal and syphilis serology was negative. Her ECG showed some T wave flattening in V4−V6, but was otherwise normal.

1. What is the diagnosis?
2. How would you confirm this?
3. What treatment would you give?

This lady presents with mild hypertension and mental changes. The mental state appears to fluctuate with disorientation, mild dementia and apparent depression. Her metabolic screen is unremarkable and neurological examination revealed no localising signs. Impaired vibration sense is a common finding in the elderly, and is usually of no significance. The previous history of hypertension is important as the long term consequences of uncontrolled hypertension include dementia, although it does not normally fluctuate. Drug therapy is a common cause of confusion in the elderly, often due to electrolyte imbalance. This, however, is not the case here and bendrofluazide is a relatively innocuous drug. However, the patient may well have fallen and sustained a head injury following an episode of postural hypotension and not reported it or forgotten about it. The normal haemoglobin and MCV makes the diagnosis of pernicious anaemia extremely unlikely. However, a serum B12 should be requested and likewise, thyroid function tests routinely performed, even though she has very little on examination to suggest thyroid disease.

The most likely diagnosis in this lady is a SUBDURAL HAEMATOMA and should be confirmed by CT BRAIN SCAN. The collection may appear as isodense with brain and may easily be missed, especially if there is no obvious midline shift or ventricular compression. If a CT brain scan is not available, a TECHNETIUM BRAIN SCAN and BILATERAL CAROTID ANGIOGRAPHY should be performed. An EEG may be normal or may show generalised flattening of electrical activity over one hemisphere. The absence of a skull fracture or history of head injury do not exclude the diagnosis and signs of raised intracranial pressure are often absent until a late stage. 15% of subdural haematomas are bilateral and may account for the non-lateralising nature of the reflex changes. Similarly, even if an isotope scan shows a unilateral lesion, bilateral angiography should still be performed.

There is probably no place for conservative management and bilateral burr holes should be performed and the clot aspirated. If the lesion is large and of long standing, a skull flap should be turned and the lesion removed piecemeal.

Case 5

A 27-year-old oil executive presented to Casualty with a severe epistaxis. He was normally well and when seen had a blood pressure of 115/75 mm Hg. The epistaxis was treated by nasal packing.

Eight weeks later he returned to Casualty looking sun-tanned, having spent a month working in the Middle East. Whilst there he had developed anorexia, fever, weight loss, with, more recently, a non-productive cough and progressive dyspnoea. In addition, he complained of pain in the left shoulder which was exacerbated by movement.

On examination, he looked unwell and had a temperature of 37.7°C. Pulse was 130 per minute and regular, of normal character. Blood pressure was 100/60 mmHg JVP + 4 cm. The cardiac apex was slightly displaced laterally, but was not hyperdynamic. On auscultation, the first heart sound could not be heard, but there was a prominent third heart sound. At the left sternal edge a short medium pitched early diastolic murmur was heard with a soft ejection systolic murmur. At the apex there was a soft mid-diastolic murmur. He was dyspnoeic at rest and had bilateral basal crepitations in his chest. There was no lymphadenopathy but his spleen could just be tipped.

Initial investigations showed: Hb 10.6 g/dl (10:6 g%), WBC 10.7 × 10⁹/l (10 700/mm³), ESR 76 mm/h. Platelets 256 × 10⁹/l (256 000/mm³), clotting studies normal. Chest X-ray showed a normal sized heart and pronounced pulmonary congestion. X-rays of his left shoulder were normal. ECG showed sinus rhythm with episodes of Wenckebach heart block. There was T-wave inversion in the left precordial leads. Echocardiogram showed a normal sized left ventricle with flutter on the anterior leaflet of the mitral valve and early mitral valve closure. Additional shadows were seen posteriorly within the aortic root during diastole. Urinalysis was negative.

1. What is the diagnosis?
2. What is the cause of his rhythm change?
3. What is the probable cause of his shoulder pain?
4. What would be your management?

This young man has the physical signs of ACUTE SEVERE AORTIC REGURGITATION, and his fever, anaemia, raised ESR and splenomegaly suggest INFECTIVE ENDOCARDITIS as the cause. His nasal packing was perhaps the source of infection.

The signs of acute severe aortic regurgitation differ from those of chronic disease. The regurgitant blood enters a non-dilated ventricle and end-diastolic pressure rises dramatically, causing early mitral valve closure as seen on the echocardiogram and recognised clinically by the absent first heart sound and the short length of the early diastolic murmur. The velocity of left ventricular contraction is not increased and hence the cardiac apex is not hyperdynamic and the pulse is of normal character. The high LVEDP means the diastolic blood pressure is not significantly lowered and the pulse pressure is not widened. His apical mid-diastolic murmur is an Austin Flint murmur, and the additional echos in the aortic root are caused by vegetations.

Rhythm disturbances are by no means rare in endocarditis of the aortic valve and are due to EXTRAVALVULAR EXTENSION OF INFECTION into the conducting tissue. Complete heart block may be produced and a pacemaker may be necessary.

A retrospective study of bacterial endocarditis showed almost half to have musculo-skeletal symptoms, usually arthralgia, myalgia or low back pain. In 27% these were amongst the first symptoms of the disease. The symptoms are perhaps due to CIRCULATING IMMUNE COMPLEXES. An infective arthritis is another, less likely, possibility with this man.

Management of this patient must include HIGH DOSE INTRAVENOUS ANTIBIOTICS started immediately after several blood cultures have been taken. He will require early AORTIC VALVE REPLACEMENT. The hazards of placing a valve into an infected position must be weighed against the risks of his continuing severe valvular incompetence and optimal timing of surgery requires experience and judgement. Post-operatively a full course of antibiotic therapy must be completed.

Case 6

A 32-year-old Eskimo had visited a brothel in Winnipeg. One week later, he developed a urethral discharge for which he treated himself with tablets obtained from a friend and departed north.

Two weeks after this he went to the settlement hospital complaining of a fever with swelling, pain and redness of his right ankle, knee and left wrist. On examination, he had a temperature of 39°C and the affected joints were tender, red and swollen with limited movement. Aspirated synovial fluid was sterile.

1. What are the two most likely diagnoses?
2. Suggest four cutaneous lesions which should be sought in making a diagnosis.
3. What are the four most useful investigations?

Skin lesions are very helpful in making a diagnosis of this case. 50% of patients with a GONOCOCCAL ARTHRITIS develop a distal SPARSE RASH OF ERYTHEMATOUS PAPULES WITH A HAEMORRHAGIC OR VESICULO-PUSTULAR CENTRE, but skin rashes are more common in REITER'S SYNDROME. The most common is a BALANITIS CIRCINATA – coalescing vesicles – of the glans penis and similar painless lesions are found in the mouth. KERATODERMA BLENNORRHAGICA is hyperkeratotic red papules found on the palms and soles of the feet. CONJUNCTIVITIS is a common association of Reiter's syndrome (and so is an iritis).

An attempt should be made to isolate a gonococcus because if the condition is left untreated with penicillin it will progress rapidly to joint destruction. Culture of synovial fluid is almost always sterile, BLOOD CULTURES are positive in only between 10% and 20% of cases. The diplococci might be seen on a URETHRAL SMEAR and URETHRAL CULTURE should be performed. Another important site for culture is the OROPHARYNX. Gonococcal complement fixation test is of little diagnostic value.

The presence of tenosynovitis in any other area apart from the achilles tendon is almost always diagnostic of gonococcal septicaemia.

Radiologically, apart from DESTRUCTIVE JOINT CHANGES in gonorrhoea, one might look for SACRO-ILIAC CHANGES and the CALCANEAL SPUR of Reiter's syndrome.

Case 7

A 41-year-old Indian woman presented with a 5-year history of persistent low back pain previously treated unsuccessfully by an orthopaedic department. Eighteen months previously she had had a partial thyroidectomy for a non-toxic goitre.

Examination failed to reveal any physical abnormalities.

Investigations showed Hb 10.0 g/dl (10 g%), serum calcium 1.9 mmol/1 (7.7 mg%), phosphate 0.74 mmol/1 (2.3 mg%), alkaline phosphatase 200 U/1. Blood urea and electrolytes normal. Serum albumin 35 g/l (3.5 g%).

1. Suggest three possible causes for her biochemical abnormality.
2. What five additional investigations are indicated?
3. What treatment would you recommend for her back pain?

The combination of hypocalcaemia and hypophosphataemia in this case points to a diagnosis of OSTEOMALACIA due to DIETARY DEFICIENCY OF CALCIUM, LACK OF VITAMIN D or INTESTINAL DISEASE WITH MALABSORPTION, such as tropical sprue, and in these conditions the alkaline phosphatase is usually elevated. Osteomalacia, which may be caused by any of these diagnoses, is particularly common in immigrants from India and Pakistan. Here there may be a multifactorial cause of dietary Vitamin D deficiency, pigmentation of skin resulting in the synthesis of less endogenous Vitamin D and calcium binding by phytate from chappatis in their diet.

Post-thyroidectomy hypoparathyroidism is rare and is usually associated with hypocalcaemia in combination with hyperphosphataemia.

Investigations must include BONE X-RAYS to determine the extent of bony involvement and BONE BIOPSY, which will show excess osteoid, is often indicated. URINARY EXCRETION of CALCIUM should be determined, although low in most cases of hypocalcaemia, it is elevated in two uncommon conditions, namely renal tubular acidosis and essential hypercalciuria. Small bowel malabsorption may be assessed by faecal fat excretion and if indicated, SMALL BOWEL BIOPSY performed. A DETAILED DIETARY HISTORY is mandatory.

Treatment should be begun with ORAL CALCIUM and $1\text{-}\alpha\text{-hydroxy-Vitamin D3}$ (this is a more potent form of Vitamin D with a shorter half-life, allowing reasonably rapid changes in dosage). BACK SUPPORT may be required temporarily to relieve the pain and dietary advice should, of course, be given.

Case 8

On a cold December day a 64-year-old street trader was brought into casualty by ambulance. His friends said he had fainted suddenly at his stall and had been unconscious for about two minutes. He had turned pale but had not fitted, gone blue or been incontinent. When he came round he was somewhat dazed but well orientated. The patient denied any warning of the faint and said that he now felt quite all right and did not want to come into hospital. He denied any previous attacks but his wife said later that he had fainted four months before while driving his Jaguar car and had done a considerable amount of damage to the car. She had been worried about him but he refused to see a doctor. He was taking no medication and smoked about 25 cigarettes a day; he liked to drink stout with his friends at the market. Fifteen years before he had had bilateral varicose vein ligations.

On examination he was conscious and well orientated. Neurological examination was entirely normal. There were no carotid bruits. Blood pressure was 170/110 mmHg. He had a normal pulse of 80 per minute. There was a systolic ejection murmur along the left sternal edge and scattered crepitations and rhonchi in the lung fields. There were no other physical signs.

Immediate investigations showed Hb 14.9 g/dl (14.9 g%), WBC 6.0 × 10^9/l (6000/mm^3), ESR 28 mm/h. Chest X-ray – minimal cardiomegaly. ECG – nonspecific T wave flattening in left ventricular leads.

1. What are the two most likely diagnoses?
2. Suggest one other possible diagnosis.
3. What would be the four most useful investigations?

This man has had two transient attacks of loss of consciousness. The history is inadequate to make an accurate diagnosis and great care must be taken to go into the details of each attack.

It is of vital importance to exclude STOKES-ADAM ATTACKS which can occur occur despite his normal ECG. This may have occurred acutely following a silent myocardial infarction and his ECG should be repeated together with CARDIAC ENZYMES. He will also need prolonged monitoring of his ECG by means of a 24 HOUR TAPE to look for rhythm disturbances.

EPILEPSY can cause transient loss of consciousness at any age. He is clearly an unreliable historian and so one cannot put too much weight on the absence of an aura. The absence of tonic and clonic phases and the lack of incontinence do not exclude the possibility of a fit. In this man's case a seizure could be alcohol related, due to cerebrovascular disease or related to a secondary bronchial carcinoma. He must have an EEG.

BRAIN STEM ISCHAEMIA is less likely without associated symptoms such as vertigo, paraesthesiae or diplopia. It could be due to direct vertebral artery disease or to bony compression. Although degenerative arterial change is the most likely cause, SYPHILIS SEROLOGY should be determined.

Postural hypotension might account for his present attack, especially as it occurred on a cold day when he may well have consumed alcohol. It would not, however, explain the first episode.

Drop attacks, where the patient falls to the ground without warning, are not associated with loss of consciousness and occur almost exclusively in females. They are, therefore, unlikely here.

Hypoglycaemia *must* be excluded in any unconscious patient, but is unlikely to cause such transient attacks.

The aortic ejection murmur, in association with a normal pulse, has no relevance to his attacks.

Case 9

A 23-year-old actress was found semiconscious by her flatmate with two empty tablet bottles on her bedside table. That morning she was known to have bought fifty aspirins and had also obtained sixty Distalgesic tablets from her doctor for a strained back. She had been seen by a friend three hours before leaving a coffee bar. On admission she was semi-comatose, there was no evidence of external injury and she was hyperventilating and sweating. Her pulse was 110 per minute, blood pressure 100/60 mmHg, chest clear. There were no abnormal signs in the abdomen or in the central nervous system and skull X-ray showed no fractures.

1. What would be the six most important points in the immediate management of this girl?
2. Suggest six complications that may arise from such an overdose.

The dangers in this case are those specific to salicylate, paracetamol and opiate poisoning, together with the potential hazards in the management of a comatose patient. Emergency treatment is aimed at maintaining the vital functions of adequate ventilation and circulation. Having insured the patency of the airways and assessed that VENTILATION IS ADEQUATE by clinical measurement and not by crude judgement, if necessary intermittent positive pressure respiration should be initiated. 100% oxygen must be given if the patient is in coma. NALOXONE reverses the central depressant effects of opiate analogues and should also be given if there is evidence of respiratory depression.

CIRCULATORY FAILURE must be treated by intravenous fluids and is monitored by pulse, blood pressure and a central venous pressure line. Basic investigations should be initiated with particular emphasis in this case on ACID-BASE STATUS. RENAL FUNCTION MUST BE ASSESSED (urea and electrolytes) and SALICYLATE AND PARACETAMOL LEVELS determined. In view of the potential hepatic toxicity of paracetamol, LIVER FUNCTION SHOULD BE MONITORED. A FORCED ALKALINE DIURESIS should be initiated if plasma salicylate levels are in excess of 40 mg% to 50 mg% since under alkaline conditions the excretion of salicylate is increased manifold.

The hazards of paracetamol poisoning are related to the formation of a metabolite that is hepato-toxic. Sulphydryl donors such as cysteamine, methionine and N-acetylcysteine, may prevent subsequent liver damage by binding to this metabolite, thereby preventing further injury to the liver. Other therapeutic procedures in this situation have been advocated, including charcoal haemoperfusion for severe cases of poisoning. However, these methods are restricted to use by a few selected centres and their efficacy is still uncertain. Complications of poisoning with these two drugs, therefore, include severe ACID-BASE AND ELECTROLYTE DISTURBANCES due to salicylates (mixed respiratory alkalosis and metabolic acidosis), DEHYDRATION, RENAL FAILURE due to circulatory failure, BLEEDING TENDENCIES due to hypoprothrombinaemia, GASTRIC EROSIONS and antiplatelet aggregation and CONVULSIONS.

With paracetamol the main hazard is severe HEPATOCELLULAR FAILURE which develops three to four days after the overdose. Renal failure may also occur.

Case 10

A 28-year-old printer was admitted to hospital severely ill. Eight days previously he had developed a painful swelling in his left axilla for which he had been prescribed ampicillin. This had continued to increase in size over the next six days, after which he became progressively more unwell with fever, anorexia and vomiting on two occasions. On questioning, he thought he had passed less urine than normal and that it had appeared concentrated. Two days before admission he had developed dyspnoea on climbing stairs. There was no significant past medical history, although he had been feeling more easily fatigued in the previous two months.

On examination he was lethargic and pale. His temperature was 38.4°C with warm peripheries. Respiratory rate, 20 per minute; blood pressure 130/90 mmHg; JVP was raised 5 cm and his pulse was 110 beats per minute and regular. The apex beat was palpable in the anterior axillary line and there was a presystolic gallop rhythm. Examination of the fundi revealed A-V nipping and vessel tortuosity. There was slight ankle oedema. In the respiratory system, extensive bilateral crepitations were heard. The other systems were normal, apart from the presence of a 6 cm × 8 cm tender, fluctuant abscess in the left axilla.

Investigations showed: Hb 8.0 g/dl (8.0 g%), MCV 80 fl (80 μ^3), MCHC 19 mmol/l (31%), WBC 18 × 10^9/l (18 000/mm^3) (92% polymorphs), platelets 220 × 10^9/l (220 000/mm^3), reticulocytes 2%. Sodium 124 mmol/l (124 mEq/l), (124 mEq/l), potassium 5.8 mmol/l (5.8 mEq/l), blood urea 56.6 mmol/l (340 mg%). MSU – 10^6 RBCs/mm^3. Protein + +. Urobilinogen – trace. Chest X-ray showed cardiomegaly and pulmonary oedema.

1. What is the diagnosis?
2. What are the two most important steps in management?

This man has acute renal failure as evidenced by a history of oliguria and a raised blood urea occurring during an acute illness. However, he also has a normochromic, normocytic anaemia and evidence of chronic hypertension. This is very suggestive of previous significant renal impairment and that the diagnosis is ACUTE ON CHRONIC RENAL FAILURE. Anaemia may occur with acute renal failure, but usually after several weeks and tends to be less severe. Severe haemolysis may in itself cause acute renal failure, but the absence of significant amounts of urobilinogen or a reticulocytosis excludes this.

His immediate problems are FLUID OVERLOAD and infection; the former, should large doses of INTRAVENOUS DIURETICS and FLUID RESTRICTION fail, will require DIALYSIS. The choice between peritoneal and haemodialysis is not clear cut, but peritoneal dialysis is effective for patients in whom fluid overload is the predominant problem and when the blood urea is not rising very rapidly. It does not require specially trained staff, but is relatively inefficient and uncomfortable, and peritonitis, chest infections, hypoalbuminaemia and hypovolaemic collapse can easily occur.

His other urgent problem is SEPSIS from his axillary abscess which in this case has probably led to septicaemia and subsequent acute tubular necrosis. This is a common presentation of chronic renal disease where the patient has undiagnosed chronic impairment, develops an intercurrent illness and is followed by a rapid deterioration in renal function. The abscess should be incised and PUS and BLOOD SENT FOR CULTURE. The most likely organism is Staphylococcus aureus and INTRAVENOUS FLUCLOXACILLIN is the drug of choice. However, until sensitivities are known, several antibiotics should be used. The acute tubular necrosis should resolve, and renal function return to its previous level. The chronic renal failure will, of course, need to be investigated in due course, but the most likely cause is chronic glomerulonephritis.

Because of his poor renal function, intravenous pyelography will not provide adequate visualisation of his urinary tract, but X-RAYS OF THE ABDOMEN WITH TOMOGRAPHY will show renal size and rule out any radio-opaque calculi. Retrograde pyelography will rule out obstructive uropathy but this is most unlikely in this case. Further investigation would include BLOOD SUGAR, SERUM CALCIUM AND URIC ACID LEVELS, SERUM PROTEINS and DNA BINDING. RENAL BIOPSY would probably enable a firm diagnosis to be made, but could be delayed until the acute tubular necrosis had resolved.

Case 11

A 64-year-old publican was admitted to hospital for investigation of anaemia. He had been a heavy drinker most of his life and smoked 20 cigarettes a day. For two months he had noted increasing shortness of breath on exertion and had felt unwell.

On examination he was clinically anaemic and bilateral Dupuytren's contractures were noted. His pulse was 66 per minute, regular rhythm, blood pressure 190/100 mmHg. There was no cardiomegaly. The heart sounds were normal and he was not in cardiac failure. The lung fields were clear.

In his abdomen the liver was enlarged 6 cm below the costal margin and was soft and not tender. The spleen was palpable 7 cm below the left costal margin.

Investigations: Hb 9.1 g/dl (9.1 g%), PCV 0.30 (30%), MCHC 18.6 mmol/l (30%), reticulocyte count 3%, WBC 9.0 × 10⁹/1 (9000/mm³), normal differential. Film – anisocytosis, polychromasia, occasional nucleated red cells. ESR 30 mm/h. Urea and electrolytes normal, platelets 190 × 10⁹/1 (190 000/mm³), plasma proteins normal. Serum bilirubin 12 μ mol/1 (0.7 mg%), aspartate transaminase 16 U/1, alanine transaminase 12 U/1, alkaline phosphatase 100 U/1. Urine: urobilinogen not increased, bilirubin negative. Direct Coombs test negative. Serum iron 17μ mol/1 (95μg%), TIBC 53 μ mol/1 (300μ g%).

1. What is the most likely type of anaemia from which this patient is suffering?
2. Give three possible diagnoses which might account for the observed findings.
3. Give the four most appropriate investigations.

This patient was thought initially to have a haemolytic anaemia following hypersplenism. However, with nucleated red cells in the peripheral blood and a normal serum bilirubin, an early ERYTHROBLASTIC ANAEMIA should be considered more probable. This is not the picture of iron deficiency in view of the normal serum iron and TIBC.

Apart from the history of alcohol and the clinical findings of hepatosplenomegaly there were no other signs to indicate chronic liver disease or the development of portal hypertension. The excessive enlargement of the spleen and the soft but grossly enlarged liver would be unusual features in cirrhosis with portal hypertension.

A RETICULOSIS, CHRONIC LEUKAEMIA or MYELOFIBROSIS could well present in this way and relevant investigations must include a STERNAL MARROW or iliac crest biopsy if necessary and a LIVER BIOPSY. LEUCOCYTE ALKALINE PHOSPHATASE and examination for PHILADELPHIA CHROMOSOME would be appropriate.

Case 12

At a company medical examination, a 58-year-old seaman was found to have marked finger clubbing and said that he had been short of breath recently and had always had a smoker's cough. He led a simple life, smoking 15 cigarettes a day, drinking quite heavily and keeping a green parrot for company. Apart from a broken leg many years before, he had never been in hospital.

On examination, the only findings were bilateral basal crepitations. He was not cyanosed and there were no cardiovascular abnormalities. His chest X-ray showed a diffuse reticular pattern at the lung bases. He was started on steroids which made no difference to his condition. Lung function tests showed:

Vital capacity	2.5 litres	Predicted normal – 3.8–4.7 litres
FEV_1	1.7 litres	Predicted normal – 2.5–3.5 litres
$FEV_1 : FVC$	68%	Predicted normal – over 75%
Total lung capacity	4.7 litres	Predicted normal – 5.5–7.3 litres
CO diffusing capacity	7.9 ml CO/min/mm Hg	Predicted normal – 27 ml CO/min/mm Hg
$PaCO_2$	5.2 kPa (39 mm Hg)	
PaO_2	9.8 kPa (74 mm Hg)	

1. Describe the pulmonary function abnormality present in this patient.
2. Give 6 possible diagnoses.
3. What would happen to the PaO_2 and $PaCO_2$ on exertion and why?
4. What would happen to the PaO_2 and $PaCO_2$ on breathing 100% oxygen and why?

The lung function tests of this man show reduced lung volumes and diffusion capacity together with slight airways obstruction probably because of smoking. This is the produce of a predominantly RESTRICTIVE VENTILATORY DEFECT and with the clinical picture and chest X-ray suggests a diagnosis of pulmonary interstitial fibrosis. There are numerous aetiologies to this disease. Extrinsic allergic factors must be sought, for example, by examining serum for AVIAN and ASPERGILLUS PRECIPITINS (note typically, the fibrosis in bird fanciers is confined to the middle and upper zones). In his job he is likely to have been exposed to a variety of noxious dusts such as ASBESTOS (silicosis usually produces an obstructive pattern of lung function tests). There is no history of drug ingestion with this man, but other causes to be considered include CRYPTOGENIC FIBROSING ALVEOLITIS, collagen disorders such as SCLERODERMA, and miscellaneous diseases such as SARCOIDOSIS (here one might have expected a response to steroid therapy and no clubbing). LYMPHANGITIS CARCINOMATOSA can give a similar picture and would fit with his long smoking history.

On exertion one would expect the PaO_2 to fall because the increased tissue utilization cannot be compensated for due to ventilation perfusion imbalance in the lung. The increased hyperventilation lowers the $PaCO_2$.

Normally, the blood flow and ventilation of lung areas is matched. With lung fibrosis this is upset so that blood still perfuses underventilated areas of lung. By breathing 100% oxygen this factor of hypoventilation is removed so that, unless there are large areas of lung tissue receiving little or no ventilation (and as such functionally indistinguishable from a right to left shunt) the PaO_2 would rise to high levels with little or no change in the $PaCO_2$ in uncomplicated diffuse interstitial pulmonary fibrosis.

Case 13

A 20-year-old American go-go dancer on holiday in London came to the casualty department with the following history. 24 hours before, her upper and lower lips had started to swell and on consultation with her GP antihistamines had been prescribed but to no avail. The swelling spread to involve the whole of the face and neck and was associated with tightness in her throat.

For the previous three years she had had intermittent localised swellings on her upper arms and lower legs which lasted two or three days. They were non-irritating and slightly pink in colour. Two years previously she had had a laparotomy for abdominal pain when an appendicitis was suspected but, at operation, a normal appendix was removed.

On examination she had gross non-pitting oedema of the face and neck. Both eyes were closed and the lips were very swollen. No rash was found. Examination of the cardiovascular, respiratory, alimentary and central nervous systems were normal. Urinalysis revealed no abnormality.

1. What further historical information would be helpful?
2. Suggest the most likely diagnosis and give one other possible diagnosis.
3. What was the cause of her abdominal pain two years before?
4. What is the immediate management of this patient?

The presentation is characteristic of ANGIONEUROTIC OEDEMA which presents with transitory episodes of localised oedema in subcutaneous and submucosal tissues. The disease may be HEREDITARY (autosomal dominant) or NON-HEREDITARY. Thus, it is important to determine whether or not there is a POSITIVE FAMILY HISTORY (the mother of this girl died at the age of 27 following laryngeal oedema and respiratory obstruction). The hereditary form of the disease is often more severe and may manifest with GASTROINTESTINAL OBSTRUCTION due to mucosal oedema. This is almost certainly the cause of the acute abdomen in this girl two years previously.

Hereditary angioneurotic oedema is associated in 85% of cases with a deficiency of C 1 esterase inhibitor. The other 15% have normal levels of a clinically inactive inhibitor. Clinical attacks are attributed to the activation of C 1, consumption of C 2 and C 4, and release of a vasoactive peptide. Attacks are often precipitated by trauma but may occur spontaneously.

Other conditions may present with oedematous swellings in various parts of the body, for example, URTICARIA. However, in these cases, which are manifestations of hypersensitivity phenomena, the lesions are accompanied by erythema and itching.

There are three aspects to treatment:

1. *The acute attack*. Although there is no definite evidence of benefit, most physicians would treat this with ADRENALINE, ANTIHISTAMINES and STEROIDS. INTUBATION or tracheostomy may be required to preserve an airway.

2. *Short term prevention*. Before traumatic procedures, especially dental therapy, patients may be given two units of fresh frozen plasma as a source of C 1 esterase inhibitor.

3. *Long term prophylaxis*. Antifibrinolytic agents such as EACA have been shown to reduce the frequency of attacks and more recently the synthetic androgen 'Danazol' has been proved highly effective with a lower incidence of side-effects. This would appear the treatment of choice, except possibly in pre-menopausal women. Local foci of infection that may precipitate attacks should be treated rapidly.

Case 14

An 82-year-old man had been admitted four times in the previous year with malaise, lethargy and extreme pallor. On each occasion he had been found to be anaemic but apart from the invariable finding of positive occult bloods, no definitive diagnosis had been made. During this period he had received several courses of oral iron and on two occasions he was transfused four pints of packed red cells. He smoked ten cigarettes a day, drank two or three whiskies each evening and ate reasonable food. On his latest admission examination revealed pallor, but no jaundice, lymphadenopathy or clubbing and no signs of chronic liver disease. His pulse was 80 per minute, regular rhythm, blood pressure 170/95 mmHg, JVP normal, the heart sounds were unremarkable and the respiratory system normal. In the abdomen the liver was enlarged 3 cm below the right costal margin and the spleen 2 cm below the left costal margin. Rectal examination was normal.

Investigations showed: Hb 7 g/dl (7 g%), WBC $6.0 \times 10^9/1$ (6000/mm³), reticulocytes 4%, ESR 25 mm/h. Blood urea and electrolytes normal. Serum iron 4.9μ mol/1 (25μ g%), total iron binding capacity 80μ mol/1 (450μ g%). Serum B12 and folate were normal. Barium swallow, meal, follow through and enema normal. Sigmoidoscopy revealed no abnormality and occult bloods were persistently positive.

1. Give four possible causes for his anaemia.
2. Give two likely causes for the splenomegaly.
3. What two further investigations would you undertake?

This man has a severe iron deficiency anaemia recurring despite several courses of oral iron therapy and associated with persistently positive occult bloods. It is likely then that he has continuing gastrointestinal blood loss. However, tests for occult blood are very sensitive and positive tests do not always indicate significant blood loss. It is also possible that he did not take his iron therapy and old people, especially if living alone, often eat badly. A DIETARY ASSESSMENT is therefore necessary. In addition, enquiry must be made about ANALGESIC INTAKE, especially aspirin, which can cause bleeding. If it is thought necessary to assess his blood loss accurately this should be done using radioactively labelled red blood cells. Malabsorption is made less likely by his normal folate level.

Despite his normal barium meal and enema, this does not exclude significant gastrointestinal pathology as lesions may be missed. His hepatosplenomegaly might indicate portal hypertension with OESOPHAGEAL VARICES or he might have a REFLUX OESOPHAGITIS which does not have to be associated with a hiatus hernia and can be clinically silent. PEPTIC ULCERATION, both benign and malignant, might be present or he might be having GASTRIC EROSIONS possibly associated with his alcohol intake. Microvascular abnormalities known as ANGIODYSPLASIA, found most frequently in the right side of the colon, are a common cause of bleeding in the elderly.

Other gastrointestinal tumours, either benign POLYPS or malignancy especially of the CAECUM, may present this way and may be notoriously difficult to detect. Less likely at this age is bleeding from a MECKEL'S diverticulum and also unlikely is hookworm infestation.

His splenomegaly could be due to PORTAL HYPERTENSION and some authors believe it can occur with SEVERE IRON DEFICIENCY ANAEMIA alone. In addition, it may be due to THROMBOSIS OF THE SPLENIC VEIN secondary to infiltration by a gastric or pancreatic neoplasm.

Further investigation should include UPPER GASTROINTESTINAL ENDOSCOPY and if necessary, COLONOSCOPY should be performed. A generalised bleeding tendency should be excluded by CLOTTING STUDIES. His barium studies should be repeated if there is any doubt as to their quality. Other possible investigations include the examination of stools for parasites, faecal fat determinations for malabsorption, a radioisotope scan for a Meckel's diverticulum and selective gastrointestinal angiography which might be the only way of picking up a local angiomatous malformation.

Case 15

A 20-year-old boy presented with transient episodes of left-sided weakness of his arm and leg which had come on over several weeks and appeared to vary in intensity. In the previous ten days he had two epileptiform seizures. He developed diabetes at the age of three and was now taking soluble insulin 32 units and PZI insulin 32 units daily. This dosage had recently been increased because of persistent glycosuria. He had noticed that he was hungry and eating more than usual.

On examination he was pale and sweating. All the abnormal physical signs were confined to the nervous system where the relevant findings were: cranial nerves normal; weakness of the left arm and left leg; increases reflexes in the left arm and leg with a left extensor Babinski response; increased tone in the left arm and leg; no sensory deficit.

Initial investigations in Outpatients that afternoon showed: urinalysis 1% glycosuria, negative protein and ketones; Hb 13.5 g/dl (13.5 g%); ESR 30 mm/h; blood sugar 4.5 mmol/l (80 mg%).

1. What four further investigations would you undertake?
2. Give four possible diagnoses.

This young man has a pure upper motor neurone lesion affecting his left side which is intermittent and has been associated with two fits. The combination of fits and his left sided signs suggest that he has a progressive structural lesion involving his right cerebral motor cortex. The intermittent nature of these episodes suggests a possible fluctuating metabolic cause. He has had his diabetes mellitus controlled with reference to his urinary glucose. However, in outpatients he has a blood sugar of 4.5 mmol/1 (80 mg%) with glycosuria, suggesting that he has a low renal threshold. HYPOGLYCAEMIA, perhaps brought about by his recent increased insulin dosage, can produce transient neurological signs such as these; in particular, it can cause epilepsy, and his sweating on presentation may well be a clue to this diagnosis. Other likely explanations are that he has an expanding space-occupying lesion in his right motor cortex; he is diabetic and thus prone to infections, and a CEREBRAL ABSCESS is a diagnosis to be considered seriously, especially with the fits. Other structural possibilities are a MENINGIOMA or GLIOMA or a VASCULAR MALFORMATION.

Investigations must include SERIAL BLOOD SUGARS throughout the day and night to exclude hypoglycaemia. SKULL X-RAY may show a shift of a calcified pineal body or the calcification in an arterio-venous malformation. An ELECTROENCEPHALOGRAM may show a localised focus with a space-occupying lesion or a more generalised disturbance in hypoglycaemia. ENHANCED COMPUTERISED AXIAL TOMOGRAPHY will show most localised structural lesions. CSF may be needed if no cause has been found to exclude infection. CAROTID ARTERIOGRAPHY may be required if a space-occupying lesion is demonstrated and can show the abnormal blood supply of a tumour and stretching and displacement of arteries and localisation of a mass in the case of other space-occupying lesions.

Case 16

A 60-year-old widow came to outpatients and gave a clear history of four transient attacks of loss of vision in her left eye over the previous two weeks which she described 'like a curtain coming down over her eye'. The attacks lasted between 5 and 10 minutes and the vision returned completely after the attack. One attack had been associated with some speech difficulty because a friend had not been able to understand what she said, but she had not noticed anything else wrong. Ten years previously she had had a peptic ulcer for which she had eventually required an abdominal operation. She was otherwise completely well and very fit for her age.

Her blood pressure was 190/110 mmHg, pulse 80 per minute, regular and of normal character. Significant findings were mild cardiomegaly and a systolic ejection murmur along the left sternal edge. There were no arterial bruits and ophthalmic and neurological examination were normal apart from an equivocal right plantar response.

Investigations showed Hb 12.7 g/dl (12.7 g%), WBC 6.3 × 10⁹/l (6300/mm³), ESR 22 mm/h. Chest X-ray: mild left ventricular hypertrophy. Urine: routine testing normal.

1. What would you look for in her fundi?
2. What would be your management and why?
3. What are the two most probable causes of her symptoms?
4. What would be the four definitive investigations?
5. What treatment is available?

This woman suffers from amaurosis fugax of her left eye, but the episode of dysarthria and the equivocal right plantar response suggest she had also suffered some cerebral ischaemia. The cause of her symptoms is likely to be recurrent emboli to the left opthalmic and middle cerebral arteries either from an atheromatous plaque in the LEFT CAROTID ARTERY, or else from a CARDIAC LESION and, if one dilates her pupils and examines the fundi carefully, one might find CHOLESTEROL EMBOLI lodged in the arterial tree. Platelet emboli can sometimes be observed in the retinal arteries during an episode of amaurosis fugax.

The suggestion of cerebral ischaemia is most significant and this patient should be ADMITTED TO HOSPITAL, as she is at a substantial risk of developing a major CVA in the near future.

A cardiac source for the emboli should be excluded by ECG, CARDIAC ENZYMES and ECHOCARDIOGRAPHY. Fragments of a calcific aortic valve can embolise occasionally and these are seen in the retinal arteries as glistening pearly white fragments, quite different from cholesterol emboli. 24 hour tape monitoring would be necessary if one suspects an arrhythmia. CAROTID ANGIOGRAPHY will define atheromatous plaques which usually lie at the bifurcation of the common carotid and do not always produce a bruit. Whilst these plaques can be removed by carotid endarterectomy, the feasibility of this depends on the general state of the patient. Most surgeons will require bilateral carotid angiography pre-operatively and as this carries some morbidity in the elderly, it is only indicated if surgery is contemplated.

If surgery is not contemplated, antiplatelet drugs (in particular, aspirin) help to prevent further emboli from an atheromatous plaque, but one must be careful in view of the previous peptic ulceration. Anticoagulation does not have any beneficial effect on carotid atheroma, but is necessary if the patient has cardiac thrombus formation.

Case 17

An 18-year-old Moroccan girl, who had arrived in England three months previously, came to the Casualty Department with a month's history of sweats, intermittent fever, weight loss and lassitude. During this time she had had intermittent lower abdominal pain and heavy periods. Three days before admission she developed a painful rash on her legs. She had taken only aspirin for the fever during this time. There was no relevant past medical history.

On examination she was pyrexial (38°C) and thin. She had raised, hot, circumscribed nodules, 3 cm to 5 cm in diameter, which were tender, on her shins, forearms and lower trunk. All other systems were normal, except that on vaginal examination she was tender in the right fornix.

1. What is the skin rash?
2. What is the most likely diagnosis?
3. Give two other possible diagnoses.
4. Give six important investigations.

This young woman has ERYTHEMA NODOSUM which may affect parts of the body other than the shins. She comes from Morocco and so TUBERCULOSIS must be high on the list of possible causes. Her only other physical sign is that she is tender on vaginal examination on the right. This, with her history of lower abdominal pain and menorrhagia, suggests pathology in her ovarian tubes or uterus. UNILATERAL SALPINGITIS can be caused by tuberculosis and is the most likely diagnosis. CROHN'S DISEASE may also present with abdominal pain and may be associated with erythema nodosum. POLYARTERITIS NODOSA can rarely also produce similar cutaneous lesions and is associated with pathology in the bowel. Other causes of erythema nodosum, such as sarcoid, ulcerative colitis and drug ingestion are not born out by the history and clinical findings.

Investigations should be primarily orientated to excluding tuberculous salpingitis and should include CHEST X-RAY and ZN STAINING AND CULTURE FOR TUBERCULOSIS of SPUTUM, URINE and HIGH VAGINAL SWAB. A DIAGNOSTIC DILATATION AND CURETTAGE may provide bacteriological or histological evidence of tuberculosis in the endometrium. A barium meal and follow-through is indicated if Crohn's disease is suspected, and investigations for polyarteritis nodosa should include anti-nuclear factor, hepatitis B antigen and appropriate biopsies.

Case 18

A middle-aged male was brought into Casualty unconscious. There were no accompanying relatives and he had been found in the local park.

On examination, his temperature was 37.8°C, blood pressure 90/70 mmHg, pulse 130 per minute, regular. His chest was clear and his abdomen was normal. Examination of his central nervous system showed that he was unresponsive to painful stimuli. His respiration was 14 per minute. His pupils were dilated, barely reacting to light. There was no meningism, tone was increased in all limbs and there were bilateral extensor plantars. The fundi were normal, and there were symmetrically brisk reflexes. General examination was unremarkable.

Investigations showed the following: Hb 13.0 g/dl (13.0 g%), WBC 13 × 10⁹/1 (13 000/mm³), platelets normal. Urea and electrolytes: sodium 131 mmol/1 (131 mEq/1), potassium 4.0 mmol/1 (4.0 mEq/1), urea 6.7 mmol/1 (40 mg%). Blood sugar 4.8 mmol/1 (86 mg%), calcium 2.32 mmol/1 (9.28 mg%). Chest X-ray showed apical fibrosis in the right lung. Skull X-ray was normal.

Examination of the CSF showed: two lymphocytes. No red cells. Gram stain negative. Protein 0.4 g/1 (40 mg%), sugar 3.8 mmol/1 (68 mg%). OP 14 cm H₂O.

ECG showed sinus tachycardia with occasional unifocal ventricular ectopics.

Shortly after the lumbar puncture he had two grand mal fits.

1. What is the diagnosis?
2. How would you confirm it?

The patient presents with a common clinical problem: a disordered state of consciousness and no available history. There are several possibilities including a post ictal state, cerebrovascular accidents including subarachnoid haemorrhage, infection either generalised or localised to the central nervous system, poor cerebral perfusion secondary to cardiac disease and, probably most common, drug overdose.

The commoner metabolic abnormalities are excluded by a normal glucose, calcium, urea and serum electrolytes. There is no evidence of meningitis and the mild leucocytosis in the peripheral blood is very non-specific and could have occurred following an unrecognised fit. Certainly for tuberculous meningitis to have caused such a disturbance of consciousness, the CSF would show some abnormality, even if AAFB were not seen.

The neurological signs do not localise any lesion and the findings of brisk reflexes, hypertonia and dilated pupils point to a generalised disturbance. In association with a sinus tachycardia and ventricular ectopics and the development of fits, a diagnosis of TRICYCLIC ANTIDEPRESSANT OVERDOSE is most likely. The severe overdose may in fact present with status epilepticus in which case the diagnosis may be delayed. The diagnosis is confirmed by IDENTIFICATION OF THE TRICYCLIC COMPOUND in PLASMA.

Treatment is supportive, with maintenance of an adequate airway and, if necessary, intubation if respiration is significantly depressed. Forced diuresis has no place in management. The treatment of arrhythmias is difficult, as most of the commoner anti-arrhythmics potentiate the cardiotoxicity of the drug. Generally, the arrhythmias in this condition appear to be fairly benign and do not need treatment. Occasionally, pacing and DC shock may be required. Coma may be reversed with the cholinesterase inhibitor, physostigmine, but it is short-acting and may precipitate convulsions and bradycardia.

Case 19

A 50-year-old Indian epileptic woman, who had been well controlled on phenytoin for many years, came to Medical Outpatients with a three month history of tiredness and a three week history of mild watery diarrhoea. In her past medical history she had had tuberculosis treated with triple chemotherapy ten years previously. Dietary assessment confirmed an adequate intake.

On examination the only abnormal findings were that she was clinically anaemic and thin.

Investigations showed: Hb 8 g/dl (8 g%), MCV 112 fl (112 μ^3), ESR 60 mm/h, serum B12 60 ng/l (60 pg/ml), serum folate 60 μg/l (60 ng/ml), faecal fats 28 mmol/24 h (8 g/24 h).

1 What is your diagnosis?
2. Suggest the six more useful investigations that should be carried out.

The woman has a megaloblastic anaemia associated with steatorrhoea. Megaloblastic anaemia may complicate phenytoin therapy due to folate deficiency, but in this case the serum folate is very high and the serum B12 low. This combination suggests a BLIND LOOP SYNDROME which occurs when there is stasis of intestinal material. It can be caused by many anatomical and functional abnormalities such as surgically created blind loops, diverticulae, internal fistulae due to Crohn's Disease or by the dilated and hypomotile intestine of scleroderma. Although she has had no previous surgery which may have led to this syndrome, she has had tuberculosis and reactivation of this disease affecting the small bowel may lead to stasis and multiplication of intestinal bacteria in the small bowel. These bacteria deconjugate bile salts, thus interfering with fat absorption and causing steatorrhoea. Deconjugated bile salts also act as irritants in the large intestine and cause diarrhoea. The syndrome may, however, be asymptomatic. To confirm the diagnosis of a blind loop syndrome, UPPER JEJUNAL INTUBATION and aspiration of the contents for culture and bacterial counts must be performed. A simple non-invasive test is the ^{14}C BREATH TEST. For this test, ^{14}C glycocholate is ingested with a Lundh test meal and the ^{14}CO$_2$ exhaled is measured. If bacterial overgrowth is present, the bacteria will deconjugate the glycocholate and release ^{14}C in the form of ^{14}CO$_2$. The urinary indicans excretion is normally raised.

UPPER INTESTINAL RADIOGRAPHY to demonstrate fistulae or obstructive lesions and a CHEST X-RAY, CULTURES OF SPUTUM, URINE AND FAECES to look for active tuberculosis should be done. A megaloblastic anaemia should be confirmed by MARROW BIOPSY and some bone marrow sent for culture. A SCHILLING TEST should be performed, which will be abnormal with and without intrinsic factor, thereby excluding pernicious anaemia as a cause of the low serum B12. Although this diagnosis would not explain the diarrhoea, it is the commonest cause of vitamin B12 deficiency and must be excluded. If a stricture is found on barium studies, laparotomy and surgical resection might be necessary.

Otherwise, treatment for the blind loop syndrome requires Tetracycline to sterilise the upper bowel, B12 supplements for the anaemia should be given and the tuberculosis should be treated by appropriate chemotherapy and prolonged follow-up.

Case 20

A 68-year-old publican presented with one month's history of anorexia, malaise and a productive cough. The latter symptom was of a week's duration, the sputum being purulent with flecks of blood.

The patient had a partial gastrectomy for a duodenal ulcer ten years ago, but the operation was only partially successful and the patient's dyspepsia often required antacids. Four years ago he had had an inferior myocardial infarction but made a good recovery.

He drank four pints of beer per day and, until his infarct, smoked 25 cigarettes a day.

On examination, he was obese. His blood pressure was 150/90 mm Hg, pulse 88 per minute and regular. He had normal heart sounds with an atrial gallop. In the chest, the percussion note was decreased at the right base, where there were coarse inspiratory crepitations. The abdomen was normal.

Investigations: Hb 11.6 g/dl (11.6 g%), WBC 9 × 10⁹/l (9000/mm³), platelets 286 × 10⁹/l (286 000/mm³), ESR 100 mm/h. Sodium 128 mmol/l (128 mEq/l), potassium 3.9 mmol/l (3.9 mEq/1), urea 4.2 mmol/1 (25 mg%), bicarbonate 25 mmol/l (25 mEq/l), aspartate transaminase 36 U/l, alkaline phosphatase 112 U/l, bilirubin 16 μ mmol/l (0.9 mg%), total protein 91 g/l (9.1 g%), albumin 28 g/l (2.8 g%), calcium 2.70 mmol/l (10.8 mg%), phosphate 1.2 mmol/l (3.7 mg%), blood sugar 6.4 mmol/l (115 mg%), cholesterol and triglycerides normal. Serum osmolality 282 mosm/kg, urinary osmolality 512 mosm/kg.

Chest X-ray showed right basal shadowing. Sputum culture grew haemophilus influenzae.

1. What is the most likely diagnosis?
2. Give five useful investigations.

This man presents with a non-specific history and a chest infection, for which there is almost certainly an underlying cause. In addition, he is mildly anaemic with a high ESR. The albumin is low and his globulins raised. He is hypercalcaemic, which is partly masked by hypoalbuminaemia and his phosphate and alkaline phosphatase are normal. This makes hyperparathyroidism and bony metastases unlikely. His hyponatraemia is not compatible with inappropriate ADH secretion, as there is no discrepancy between his serum osmolality (which is normal) and urine. In fact, he has a pseudohyponatraemia with a normal sodium concentration relative to a normal plasma water. However, in hyperlipidaemic or hyperproteinaemic states, the normal method for assaying sodium and calculating OSMOLARITY are invalidated. In view of his normal lipids and a raised total serum protein, hyperglobulinaemia seems likely. Taken with the hypercalcaemia, MULTIPLE MYELOMA is the likeliest diagnosis.

Investigations should include IMMUNOGLOBULINS, PLASMA PROTEIN ELECTROPHORESIS, SKELETAL SURVEY, examination of the URINE for BENCE-JONES PROTEIN and BONE MARROW BIOPSY.

His chest infection, which cleared with antibiotics, could have caused hyponatraemia, as could a bronchial carcinoma. Hypercalcaemia due to milk alkali syndrome is accompanied by an alkalosis.

Case 21

A 34-year-old English housewife was brought into Casualty severely ill. Her husband said that over the last month she had been unwell, short of breath, her ankles swollen and stomach distended. She was epileptic and took phenobarbitone irregularly for this. Two years before, her chest X-ray had been normal at a routine medical examination. She had never been pregnant, and had no chest pain, fever or joint pains.

When examined she had massive oedema, ascites and a pleural effusion. The liver was palpable 2 cm below the costal margin. The blood pressure was unrecordable, pulse 130 per minute, JVP elevated to her ears, more prominent on inspiration. The heart sounds were faint, a third sound present, and there was no palpable apex beat.

Investigations: chest X-ray – bilateral pleural effusions, large cardiac shadow; ECG – sinus rhythm, low voltage with electrical alternans of axis; Hb 13.8 g/dl (13.8 g%), WBC 17 × 10⁹/l (17 000/mm³), ESR 20 mm/h, urea 7.6 mmol/l (46 mg%), plasma sodium 135 mmol/l (135 mEq/l), potassium 3.8 mmol/l (3.8 mEq/l), serum proteins and immunoglobulins normal; Rose-Waaler, latex and anti-nuclear factor negative, ASOT normal; T4 and T3 normal; rectal biopsy normal.

1. What are the three most likely causes of her illness?
2. What are the three most useful investigations?

This woman presents with the signs of cardiac tamponade, presumably secondary to a pericardial effusion. The presence of the effusion would be confirmed by an ECHOCARDIOGRAM which would show an echo free space behind the left ventricle and/or in front of the right ventricle. On admission, 750 ml of blood stained fluid was removed by pericardial tap and she improved on medical treatment. However, over the next few weeks her tamponade returned and her condition deteriorated rapidly. She had several PERICARDIAL TAPS and specimens taken for CULTURE AND CYTOLOGY were normal.

A VIRAL AETIOLOGY was thought likely, but VIRAL ANTIBODY SCREENING to a wide range of viruses was negative. TUBERCULOUS PERICARDITIS is possible, but her MANTOUX REACTION was negative at 1 in 100, making the diagnosis very unlikely. In addition, tubercle bacilli were not grown from the pericardial fluid, although this only occurs in 50% of cases. A PRIMARY or SECONDARY TUMOUR OF THE PERICARDIUM is a possibility.

Myxoedema and uraemia have been excluded on biochemical grounds and a collagen disorder is also unlikely on the history and laboratory findings. Amyloid is a rare cause of a pericardial effusion, but her rectal biopsy was normal. She is old for rheumatic fever and has no other suggestive clinical features. Acute benign pericarditis is likewise unlikely in view of the severity of her illness and lack of constitutional symptoms.

Because of her recurrent pericardial effusions, surgical exploration and excision of the pericardium was performed. The histology showed masses of anaplastic cells and six months later she died from her ovarian carcinoma.

The changing electrical axis of the ECG is due to the heart swinging about in the bag of fluid. It has been said that if the P, QRS and T waves all show alternans, this is virtually diagnostic of cardiac tamponade.

Case 22

A 35-year-old man was admitted to casualty unconscious; he had been found lying in the road by a group of people leaving a pub. No history was available but a card was found in his pocket stating that he was an epileptic and was taking phenytoin (Epanutin) and phenobarbitone. A hospital attendance card was also found which showed that he had been started on anti-epileptic drugs only two years before.

On examination he was dirty, unkempt and smelt of alcohol; there were no needle marks on his arms. His temperature was 37.4°C. The other abnormalities were confined to the nervous system. He was unconscious but responded to painful stimuli. The cranial nerves were normal. He had generalised spasticity with symmetrical hyper-reflexia and flexor plantar responses. A skull X-ray showed no fractures. He improved initially, and was able to respond to commands for a period of over six hours, but suddenly became deeply unconscious with fixed dilated pupils, neck rigidity and extensor plantar responses.

1. What do you think is the differential diagnosis of coma on admission? Give four possibilities.
2. What do you think caused his subsequent deterioration after six hours and what two important diagnostic investigations must be carried out?

The differential diagnosis of his coma on admission is wide. He is an epileptic and could be in POST ICTAL COMA. He might have sustained a HEAD INJURY during a fit. He is on anti-epileptic drugs and could have taken an OVERDOSE of these or ALCOHOL or a combination of both. Initial examination revealed no focal neurology then suddenly after six hours of improvement he deteriorates rapidly. The acuteness of his deterioration and physical signs suggest either a SUBARACHNOID HAEMORRHAGE or herniation of the cerebellar tonsils due to raised intracranial pressure. While the former is more likely, the presence of an intracranial mass causing the latter must be excluded by a BRAIN SCAN. However, the combination of epilepsy of late onset and subarachnoid haemorrhage points to an ARTERIO-VENOUS MALFORMATION. It is most unusual for such rapid deterioration with a subdural haemorrhage and his initial improvement makes a drug overdose unlikely. It is imperative to substantiate the diagnosis of subarachnoid haemorrhage at this stage by performing a LUMBAR PUNCTURE and obtaining CSF. Most neurosurgeons would not undertake INTRACRANIAL ANGIOGRAPHY with the patient deeply unconscious, as operative intervention in this situation carries a similar mortality to allowing the disease to take its natural course. However, if he subsequently improves, angiography should be performed.

The diagnosis of the underlying pathology might have been suspected on examination by the finding of a cranial bruit, on initial skull X-ray by the finding of tram-line calcification, and confirmed by the delineation of the arterio-venous malformation on cranial arteriography.

Case 23

A 43-year-old university lecturer was referred to Medical Outpatients because of recurrent headaches. These tended to occur at any time of the day, were throbbing in nature, situated at the vertex and frontal regions and lasted for between 5 minutes and an hour. The attacks had started 4 months previously and initially had occurred at 3 or 4 week intervals; however in the past month the attacks had occurred every four or five days. The headaches did not respond to aspirin, but the patient often experienced central abdominal pain and nausea during an attack and sometimes sweating. There were no visual symptoms either before or during an attack and there were no sensory symptoms in the limbs. He was on no regular medication and there was no significant past medical history.

Examination revealed a fit looking man. Blood pressure was 130/90 mmHg supine and 95/60 mmHg standing; pulse 78 beats per minute and regular. There were no abnormalities in the heart, chest or abdomen. Examination of the central nervous system showed normal power, tone and sensation in all limbs. All reflexes were brisk and equal and both plantar responses were flexor. The cranial nerves were normal. Fundoscopy showed a small flame-shaped haemorrhage in the inferior temporal quadrant of the left eye and some arterial irregularity. There was no evidence of papilloedema.

Investigations showed: Hb 15.8 g/dl (15.8 g%), WBC 8.4 X 10^9/1 (8400/mm^3), ESR 40 mm/h. Urea and electrolytes, liver function tests and serum calcium were normal. Random blood sugar was 12.8 mmol/1 (230 mg%). VDRL was negative; MSU was sterile. The chest and skull X-rays were normal, as was the brain scan. Barium meal and follow through showed no abnormality. Intravenous pyelography suggested flattening of the upper calyx of the left kidney. The upper pole of both kidneys was opposite the upper border of the 12th thoracic vertebrae. The ureter and bladder outlined normally.

1. What is the diagnosis?
2. How would you confirm this?

Headache is a common presenting symptom and the causes include the common 'tension' headache, migraine, temporal arteritis and cases of raised intracranial pressure due to a tumour. The clinical features of this patient's headaches are not particularly characteristic of any of these and in addition he has gastrointestinal symptoms and sweating. He is normotensive and on no medication, yet he has a degree of orthostatic hypotension. He also has mild diabetes and this could account for the haemorrhage in his left eye. Another possibility, however, is that he has had paroxysmal attacks of severe hypertension causing his headaches, which with the hyperhidrosis, suggests a diagnosis of PHAEOCHROMO-CYTOMA. The abdominal pain is a frequent symptom in paroxysmal episodes and may be due to bowel ischaemia – similar symptoms are seen in other states of increased adrenergic activity, e.g. clonidine withdrawal. Paroxysmal hypertension occurs in 40–50% of patients with phaeochromocytoma and the patient may be hypotensive following an acute episode (which often causes further delay in diagnosis). An alternative explanation for orthostatic hypotension is reduced plasma volume; however, recent studies have failed to confirm this finding in most patients with phaeochromocytoma.

Because the left kidney is normally higher than the right, the appearances on pyelography are suggestive of a suprarenal mass compressing the left kidney. There is now no place for potentially dangerous provocative tests (e.g. intravenous histamine) and diagnostic reduction of blood pressure with phentolamine has resulted in deaths from precipitous hypotension. URINARY VANILLYL-MANDELIC ACID (VMA) and METANEPHRINES are widely accepted as screening procedures, although false positives and false negatives are commonly found. PLASMA CATECHOLAMINE levels are almost invariably raised, but the patient should be resting and preferably not on vasodilator drugs, to avoid a spurious increase in plasma catecholamine levels. Multiple tumours occur in 10% of adults and a search for these should be made. Localisation of tumours with flush aorthography and renal arteriography, vena caval sampling, or CT scanning should be performed. Careful chest screening may exclude posterior mediastinal tumours.

Careful preoperative preparation, skilful anaesthesia and an experienced surgeon are vital for the surgical removal of the tumour.

Case 24

A lady of 24 went to her GP saying that for the previous two or three weeks she had felt feverish and unwell with a sore throat. Apart from a tonsillitis, the only abnormal finding was a slightly tender enlarged gland in the neck. She was started on ampicillin but stopped this two days later because of a skin rash. She continued to feel generally unwell over the next two weeks and returned to see her doctor who found: Hb 10.1 g/dl (10.1 g%), WBC 7.0×10^9/l (7000/mm^3), (2% atypical monocytes), platelets 155×10^9/l (155 000/mm^3), ESR 35 mm/h.

She was treated with iron and multivitamins but continued to deteriorate and became weaker. Three weeks later when she was admitted to hospital, her blood count was: Hb 4.5 g/dl (4.5 g%), WBC 2.0×10^9/l (2000/mm^3), platelets 90×10^9/l (90 000/mm^3).

There was no lymphadenopathy and no abnormal physical signs.

1. What is the likely diagnosis of her initial symptoms?
2. What test or tests would confirm this diagnosis?
3. What haematological complications of this disease are recognised?
4. What is the most likely explanation of the haematological abnormality three weeks after presentation and how would you investigate it?

The history of a sore throat and malaise in a young person, followed by a drug sensitivity rash on being given ampicillin, is very suggestive of INFECTIOUS MONONUCLEOSIS. The presence of atypical monocytes supports this diagnosis, as would the presence of heterophil antibody shown by the PAUL-BUNNELL test. The appearance of such antibodies might be delayed and hence an initial negative test should be repeated. Rarely the test remains negative and occasionally false positives occur. More specific, although less readily available, is the demonstration of ANTIBODIES to the E-B VIRUS shown by FLUORESCENT ANTIBODY STAINING of transformed lymphocytes. A rising titre or, with a single specimen, the presence of specific IgM antibodies may be accepted as diagnostic.

Negative results should raise the possible alternative diagnosis of infection with cytomegalovirus or Toxoplasma gondii, although in neither case would tonsillitis be expected as a prominent symptom.

Patients with infectious mononucleosis usually have a platelet count that is normal or slightly reduced. Rarely THROMBOCYTOPENIA sufficient to cause haemorrhage occurs. Another rare complication is the development of an ACUTE HAEMOLYTIC ANAEMIA which is sometimes associated with the cold antibody anti-i.

Her blood picture three weeks after presentation shows a pancytopenia. In the absence of splenomegaly the likely diagnosis is either a SUB-LEUKAEMIC LEUKAEMIA or an APLASTIC ANAEMIA. Less likely would be systemic lupus erythematosus, non-leukaemic bone marrow infiltration or disseminated tuberculosis. An aplastic anaemia could have a post-viral aetiology; this is best documented following infectious hepatitis but cases have been described following infectious mononucleosis or other viral infections. In addition, an enquiry should be made about exposure to drugs or toxins – she could, for example, have started taking cotrimoxazole and have a sulphonamide induced aplasia. Ampicillin is not usually associated with haematological complications. The diagnosis should be made by BONE MARROW ASPIRATION.

Two years later this girl died from acute myeloblastic leukaemia. Her infectious mononucleosis was a coincidental infection.

Case 25

A 14-year-old girl presented to her local GP having felt unwell for ten days during which time she had a fever, developed a transient rash on her trunk and subsequently developed pain and tenderness in her left knee. He referred her to hospital where she was admitted.

On examination, her temperature was 38.5°C. She had non-tender cervical lymphadenopathy. Her blood pressure was 120/80 mmHg, JVP not raised, pulse 110 per minute regular, the heart sounds were normal and her chest was clear. In her abdomen her splenic tip was palpable. Her left knee was swollen, tender and hot.

Initial investigations showed: Hb 12 g/dl (12 g%), WBC 13 × 10^9/l (13 000/mm^3), ESR 90 mm/h, urine microscopy showed no protein or cells.

Over the next four days she developed a swinging fever, painful wrists and pain in the neck on movement. On the fourth day she was found to have a pericardial friction rub but no murmurs and no evidence of cardiac failure. She later developed a red and painful left eye.

1. What would have been the three most likely diagnoses on admission?
2. What three important diagnostic investigations should have been carried out on admission?
3. With her subsequent course in mind, give the two most likely diagnoses.
4. How might her skin rash have helped establish the diagnosis?

The initial presentation with fever, pain and swelling of the left knee and a short prodromal history makes it imperative to rule out INFECTIVE ARTHRITIS or OSTEOMYELITIS, and JOINT ASPIRATION with microscopy and culture of the aspirate must be performed. BLOOD CULTURES must be taken. Sometimes ACUTE LEUKAEMIA will simulate a pyogenic arthritis, and a PERIPHERAL BLOOD FILM was made on admission. Her subsequent course suggests a systemic disease. Rubella may be associated with arthritis, a history of rash and the presence of cervical lymphadenopathy, but it is not associated with pericarditis. The important differential diagnoses lie between RHEUMATIC FEVER, STILL'S DISEASE, SYSTEMIC LUPUS ERYTHEMATOSUS and RHEUMATOID ARTHRITIS. She is in the right age group for Still's disease and rheumatic fever, while young for SLE. The differentiation of rheumatic fever and Still's disease may be difficult as both have prodromal rashes (typically ERYTHEMA MARGINATUM or MACULO-PAPULAR), however, cervical spine involvement is more common in Still's disease, as is swinging pyrexia, lymphadenopathy and hepatosplenomegaly.

Important investigations in this patient must include SEROLOGY FOR RHEUMATOID FACTOR, ANTI-NUCLEAR FACTOR and DNA BINDING, an ECG to assess cardiac involvement, X-rays of involved joints and a chest X-ray. A full blood count and ESR, throat swab and an ASO titre should also be performed.

It is important to examine the eyes of patients with suspected Still's disease with a slit-lamp to pick up iritis as this can be a serious complication and lead to blindness. The treatment of Still's disease includes bed rest as long as systemic symptoms are present, maintenance of good alignment of joints with splints and physiotherapy to maintain muscle function. Aspirin should be given for symptomatic relief.

Case 26

A 32-year-old insulin-dependent diabetic woman taking 24 units of soluble and 20 units of lente insulin daily presented in Casualty following a fainting episode. She had had previous similar episodes over the past week. On examination she was found to be 28 weeks pregnant and there were no focal neurological signs. The urine showed 1% glycosuria. On further questioning, it was ascertained she had not booked for this pregnancy.

1. Suggest three reasons that would account for her fainting.
2. What three investigations are indicated?
3. What would your further management of this woman be?

The most likely cause of this woman's recurrent fainting attacks is undoubtedly HYPOGLYCAEMIA, despite the persistance of glycosuria, which reflects only the lowered renal threshold for glucose in pregnancy. Insulin requirements usually rise in the second and third trimester of pregnancy, though hard and fast rules cannot be depended upon and she is on a combination regime each morning, which is unlikely to give good diabetic control. Other causes of faints peculiar to pregnancy should be considered. These episodes might have been due either to POSTURAL HYPOTENSION, ANAEMIA, or ECLAMPTIC FITS associated with toxaemia.

It is imperative that this woman be admitted to hospital immediately. A BLOOD SUGAR SERIES should be performed and her diabetes controlled on twice or thrice daily short-acting insulin. RENAL FUNCTION should be assessed and the WELLBEING OF THE FETUS ALSO ASSESSED by serial ultrasounds and oestriol levels.

Further management of the diabetic pregnancy would depend on the presence of any complicating factor. However, once her diabetes is well controlled and there are no complicating factors and the fetus continues to grow, the patient could be discharged. She would manage her own diabetes mellitus, measuring blood sugars at home using a meter or accurate glucose oxidase strips. She could then be readmitted at 37–38 weeks to be induced. Following delivery, insulin requirements usually revert to pre-pregnancy levels.

Case 27

A 19-year-old typist presented with a four day illness of fever, sweating, pain and weakness in the left shoulder and left upper arm. Two weeks previously she had a three day episode of lower abdominal pain associated with a vaginal discharge, for which she had been prescribed ampicillin by her GP. She had been referred to a VD clinic, but no evidence of venereal infection had been found. She had no past medical history of any serious illnesses.

On examination she had a pyrexia of 39.5°C and was obviously ill. There was severe pain and localised tenderness over the left scapula and left humerus where firm red swellings were palpable. Movement of the arm was severely restricted by pain. The skin was hot and reddened and fasciculation was noted.

Investigations showed: Hb 13.0 g/dl (13 g%); WBC $14 \times 10^9/1$ (14 000/mm³); ESR 70 mm/h. X-ray of the chest, shoulder joint and humerus showed no abnormalities. EMG showed polyphasic potentials with increased insertion activity.

1. Give two possible diagnoses.
2. Give four further investigations.

The findings in this girl of fever, associated with discrete painful swellings in the left shoulder and arm and a leucocytosis suggest a bacterial infective aetiology. In view of the previous pelvic episode, which was possibly an acute salpingitis, a resultant SEPTICAEMIA WITH FOCAL INFECTIVE LESIONS is likely. However, an ACUTE POLYMYOSITIS could present in this way, and in this condition areas of necrotic muscle may clinically resemble abscesses. This patient did have a septicaemia and Staphylococcus aureus was cultured from the lesions, were surrounded by necrotic muscle producing EMG recordings typical of a polymyositis. Trichinosis is a rare cause of severe muscle pain and may cause oedema of affected muscles.

Investigations in this patient should include BLOOD CULTURE, ASPIRATION AND CULTURE OF THE LESIONS, A HIGH VAGINAL SWAB, measurement of SERUM CREATININE KINASE and MUSCLE BIOPSY. Skin tests and complement fixation may be of use in the diagnosis of trichinosis.

Treatment of the septicaemia would depend on the organisms isolated and in this case, cloxacillin was prescribed after drainage of the abscesses. In an acute polymyositis, steroids are indicated.

Case 28

A 30-year-old woman presented to a medical outpatient clinic complaining that she had noticed for the last five days a painful swelling in her neck. She had no other symptoms and had taken several Anadin® tablets to relieve the discomfort. She had recently had an upper respiratory tract infection and been treated with cough linctus by her GP. There were no other relevant features in her past medical history.

On examination she appeared well. She was pyrexial (38.4°C) and the thyroid was diffusely enlarged and tender.

1. What is the diagnosis?
2. What would be the result of the thyroid function test and a radio iodine uptake?
3. What treatment is indicated and what is the prognosis?

The most likely cause of the sudden development of a painful enlargement of the thyroid gland in the absence of any previous history of thyroid disease is DE QUERVAIN'S THYROIDITIS.

Thyroid function tests would frequently show ELEVATION OF SERUM THYROXIN and TRI-IODOTHYRONINE associated with a LOW RADIO IODINE UPTAKE. Thyroid antibodies are normally negative and the aetiology of this condition is thought probably to be due to virus infection. Occasionally, NEEDLE BIOPSY OF THE THYROID GLAND is needed to exclude thyroid carcinoma when tenderness is not marked and the gland is hard.

Often no treatment is required other than mild analgesia. In severe cases, prednisolone (20–30 mg daily) causes symptomatic relief. The course is variable, but usually complete recovery is the rule.

Case 29

A 64-year-old businessman went to see his general practitioner accompanied by his wife. She stated that she had become increasingly worried about her husband who was often drowsy during the daytime and whose previously successful business was beginning to founder. The man denied these difficulties but did state that he had had difficulty in sleeping recently and that his ankles had become swollen. He had previously been well except for a hospital admission 5 years ago with a small, uncomplicated myocardial infarction. He admitted to smoking 5 cigars per day and to drinking at business lunches with an additional whisky as a night-cap.

The family doctor advised him to take a holiday and prescribed nitrazepam at night for his insomnia, frusemide for his swollen ankles and Feospan as a general tonic, as he thought the man looked pale.

A month later the man was brought into Casualty having been very confused and aggressive that morning. He had apparently initially improved following his medication but more recently his ankle oedema had returned and he had increased his diuretic therapy himself. In the three days before admission he had become increasingly confused and drowsy.

On examination, he looked pale and had bilateral Dupuytren's contractures. His abdomen was distended with dullness in both flanks and there was bruising on both legs. Rectal examination revealed a black stool. Neurologically, the man was stuporose, being rousable by pain, muscle tone increased, his tendon reflexes all symmetrically exaggerated and both plantar responses extensor. No sensory loss could be found.

Initial investigations showed: Hb 13.4 g/dl (13.4 g%), MCV 104 fl (104 μ^3), WBC 12 × 10^9/l (12 000/mm^3), salicylate and paracetamol screens negative, glucose 4.7 mmol/l (85 mg%), sodium 132 mmol/l (132 mEq/l), potassium 2.9 mmol/l (2.9 mEq/l), urea 2.0 mmol/l (12 mg%). Chest and skull X-rays normal. ECG showed an old inferior myocardial infarction.

1. What is the likely diagnosis?
2. Name 5 factors that may have caused his deterioration.
3. Name 6 important principles in management.

This man presents with confusion and drowsiness and on examination there is evidence of ascites and purpura. Although disseminated malignancy with abdominal and intracerebral secondaries, could give a similar picture, his raised MCV and Dupuytren's contractures point towards an alcoholic aetiology. Patients often do not tell their true alcohol consumption. His neurological state is consistent with HEPATIC ENCEPHALOPATHY which can be of insidious onset. The most characteristic (but not diagnostic) sign the casualty officer should elicit would be asterixis (or flapping tremor). In anyone with neurological deterioration who might have been falling (bruises), it is important to exclude a subdural haematoma.

Deterioration of this man's encephalopathy may be due to:
a. A recent alcoholic binge.
b. Gastrointestinal haemorrhage – his black stool may be due to his iron therapy, but he might also have melaena.
c. Electrolyte imbalance (hypokalaemia or hyponatraemia) due to his frusemide.
d. His nitrazepam treatment – people in encephalopathy have increased susceptibility to sedatives.
e. Infection, which should be avidly looked for – especially septicaemia and infected ascites.

His management must include:
a. The avoidance of sedation, if at all possible.
b. Correction of electrolyte imbalance.
c. Curtailment of dietary protein.
d. Oral neomycin to reduce the colonic bacterial content.
e. Vitamin K, if necessary, to attempt to correct clotting abnormalities.
f. Treatment of infection or gastrointestinal haemorrhage, if applicable.
g. Cimetidine is useful to help prevent gastrointestinal haemorrhage.

Case 30

A 77-year-old spinster was admitted to hospital with a ten day history of vomiting, abdominal pain and dysuria. She had been treated initially with cotrimoxazole (Septrin): when she showed no response to this she was given a subsequent course of tetracycline. She was a late onset diabetic controlled by chlorpropamide 250 mg daily and a diet. During the last two or three days before admission she had 2% glycosuria but no ketonuria.

In her past medical history she had had intermittent urinary tract infections which normally responded to treatment. Thirty years ago she had had a left nephrectomy following a car accident. The only other fact of note was that she had suffered for many years from frequent headaches for which she took proprietary analgesics.

On examination, her temperature was 38.5°C, and she had a healing erythematous rash on her arms. Her blood pressure was 180/100 mmHg and there were grade II hypertensive changes in the retinal vessels. The rest of the examination was normal.

Initial investigations showed: Hb 11.0 g/dl (11 g%), blood urea 41.5 mmol/1 (250 mg%), plasma sodium 130 mmol/1 (130 mEq/1), potassium 5.0 mmol/1 (5.0 mEq/1), MSU: growth of E. coli sensitive to nalidixic acid.

She was treated with nalidixic acid to which she responded well and a week later she was symptom free and her blood urea was 18.5 mmol/1 (110 mg%).

Three weeks later she developed a further attack of pain and dysuria and suddenly developed anuria.

1. Suggest two ways in which the drug therapy has contributed to her renal failure.
2. How might the antibiotics have influenced her diabetic control?
3. Suggest two other possible causes for her anuria.

This woman has multiple pathology and has been receiving a whole range of therapeutic agents. She has a history of recurrent urinary tract infections associated with impaired renal function. Her blood urea is 41.5 mmol/1 (250 mg%) on admission and this falls to 18.5 mmol/1 (110 mg%) after a week of treatment with nalidixic acid. It is likely that the rise in blood urea is due to treatment with TETRACYCLINE causing protein catabolism. ANALGESIC ABUSE, phenacetin especially, may give rise to papillary necrosis and renal failure.

Her erythematous rash may be due to treatment with cotrimoxazole or chlorpropamide. The COMBINATION of CHLORPROPAMIDE and COTRIMOXAZOLE may give rise to a hypoglycaemic attack due to the cotrimoxazole potentiating the hypoglycaemic drug.

The most likely cause of her anuria is PAPILLARY NECROSIS, especially as she has many of the predisposing factors, namely diabetes mellitus, recurrent urinary tract infections and analgesic abuse. Septicaemia often causes acute tubular necrosis, but anuria in this condition is extremely rare. The diagnosis of papillary necrosis could be made on an INTRAVENOUS PYELOGRAM, where irregular calyces or, more rarely, calyceal ring shadows represent sloughed papillae.

The anuria suggests ureteric obstruction. RETROGRADE PYELOGRAPHY would be required to exclude bilateral ureteric calculi (or in this case a stone in the ureter of a single functioning kidney). Crystal deposition of sulphonamides is a possibility but she had not taken any for a month and only subsequently developed anuria. A third possibility in patients with pre-existing renal disease is that, rarely, ACUTE PYELONEPHRITIS itself may cause anuria.

Case 31

A 67-year-old housekeeper was admitted via Casualty. She was a heavy smoker and had recently returned from a holiday on a farm in South Wales. Three weeks before admission she had had an episode of flu with malaise and some shortness of breath. One week later she suddenly became breathless but this was treated with antibiotics and gradually subsided. Three days before admission she again became breathless and had had increasing breathlessness since. She had had no cough, haemoptysis or pleuritic chest pain.

On examination, she was afebrile. She became dyspnoeic on minimal exertion, but was not cyanosed or clubbed. Pulse 120/minute and regular, blood pressure 120/90 mmHg. Her JVP was + 6 cm and she had a parasternal heave with a gallop rhythm at the left sternal edge. Chest expansion was good and symmetrical and her chest was clinically clear.

Blood gases on admission were: pH 7.47; $PaCO_2$ 3 kPa (21 mmHg); PaO_2 8.7 kPa (65 mmHg); Bicarbonate 17.3 mmol/l (173 mEq/l).

1. What is the most likely diagnosis?
2. What would you expect the chest X-ray and ECG to show?
3. How would you confirm your diagnosis?
4. What predisposing factors would you look for?
5. What treatment would you give?

This lady presents with sudden attacks of breathlessness and has no abnormal signs in her lungs. The diagnosis of RECURRENT PULMONARY EMBOLI is therefore suggested and is compatible with the clinical findings and blood gases. Other causes of acute breathlessness include spontaneous pneumothorax, bronchospasm, pulmonary oedema and bronchial occlusion, none of which fit with the clinical findings. Hysterical hyperventilation would not cause her raised venous pressure or her low arterial oxygen tension.

The chest X-ray is likely to show little other than possible diminished vascular markings. The wedge-shaped shadows of pulmonary infarction occur with smaller emboli that present with pleuritic chest pain and haemoptysis. The ECG may show the classical S1 Q3 T3 pattern together with 'right ventricular strain' with T inversion in the right sided chest leads. More rarely right bundle branch block may occur.

The diagnosis is best confirmed by SIMULTANEOUS VENTILATION/PERFUSION LUNG SCANS. PULMONARY ARTERIOGRAPHY is required if the patient is sufficiently ill for pulmonary embolectomy to be required, or should there still be any diagnostic difficulty.

Predisposing factors include RECENT SURGERY, CONGESTIVE CARDIAC FAILURE, IMMOBILITY, INFECTION, BLOOD DYSCRASIA and MALIGNANCY. In particular, PELVIC PATHOLOGY should be excluded which might obstruct the pelvic veins causing thromboses.

She should be treated with HEPARIN and later ORAL ANTICOAGULANTS. Should her condition deteriorate then she should be transferred to a centre where pulmonary embolectomy can be performed if necessary. Streptokinase or other fibrolytic agents cause more rapid lysis of the embolus than heparin and may be infused through a catheter left in the pulmonary artery after angiography. Its use, however, has a greater risk of haemorrhage than heparin therapy.

Case 32

A 30-year-old insurance broker felt unwell and lost his appetite on returning from a three week holiday in India. He developed flatulence and abdominal discomfort after food with, a few days later, diarrhoea. Four weeks later he went to see his doctor as his symptoms were continuing and he lost a stone and a half in weight. He described his stools as pale and offensive. There was nothing of note in his past medical history.

On examination he was thin and pale. His abdomen was slightly distended although liver, spleen and kidneys were not palpable. His bowel sounds were increased. On rectal examination soft, shiny grey faeces were found and no abnormal masses were palpable. Sigmoidoscopy was normal.

Investigations: Hb 9.0 g/dl; urea and electrolytes normal; glucose tolerance test showed a flat curve; chest X-ray normal; barium meal and follow through showed a slightly dilated small bowel with coarse mucosal folds and some flocculation of the barium; 24 hour faecal fat 31.5 mmol/24 h (9 g/24 h); culture of faeces for Salmonella, Shigella and Campylobacter negative.

1. Name 3 likely diagnoses.
2. What further investigations would you perform to differentiate these?

This man has malabsorption, steatorrhoea and anaemia associated with four weeks' ill health after his return from India. His sigmoidoscopy was normal and his barium follow through showed changes compatible with his malabsorption with no other structural lesion. Infestations with protozoa and helminths are not uncommonly acquired in this geographical area and the most likely causing this picture, would be GIARDIASIS. This often causes an acute episode of diarrhoea which may merge into a chronic picture. It may be associated with a malabsorption syndrome although the aetiological significance of the Giardia has not been proven. Other parasitic infections that may cause steatorrhoea include strongyloidiasis and capillariasis (usually contracted in the Philippines). Ancylostomiasis (hookworm) may cause rapid and severe iron deficiency anaemia, but rarely malabsorption. The two other important differential diagnoses are TROPICAL SPRUE and ADULT COELIAC DISEASE. With tropical sprue the visit abroad need only be brief and may be sometime before the onset of symptoms. Less likely causes, in view of the lack of specific radiological features, would be Crohn's disease, lymphoma or intestinal tuberculosis and rare causes of malabsorption are Whipples disease and some collagen disorders. The abnormal glucose absorption makes liver, biliary or pancreatic disease unlikely.

EXAMINATION OF THE FAECES FOR PARASITES is mandatory in this case. A FULL BLOOD COUNT and FILM, SERUM IRON AND IRON BINDING CAPACITY and SERUM B12 and RED CELL FOLATE should be performed. If parasites are not isolated from his faeces then a SMALL INTESTINAL BIOPSY should be performed. At the same time, DUODENAL FLUID should be ASPIRATED for parasites and these should also be sought on an imprint of the mucosal biopsy on a slide. The histological differentiation of coeliac disease and tropical sprue may be very difficult.

Even when giardiasis has been diagnosed it should not be accepted as the sole cause of malabsorption. The response to treatment, usually metronidazole, should be closely followed and further investigations performed if necessary.

Case 33

The patient was a 16-year-old male who was admitted with the following history: for the previous six months he had complained of a generalised weakness to such an extent that he was unable to play football at school. He had no other symptoms until the day before admission, when he felt generally unwell and had vomited on one occasion.

On examination, he was noted to be small for his age (below the 3rd centile for height and weight), but sexual development was normal. The remainder of the examination was unremarkable. The blood pressure was 100/70 mmHg.

Investigations were as follows: Hb 14.0 g/dl (14 g%), WBC 6.0 × 10⁹/l (6000/mm³). Plasma sodium 135 mmol/l (135 mEq/l), potassium 2.3 mmol/l (2.3 mEq/l), bicarbonate 32 mmol/l (32 mEq/l), urea 5.3 mmol/l (32 mg%). Plasma renin activity 12 ng/ml/h (high). Urine sodium 69 mmol/24 (69 mEq/24 h), potassium 29 mmol/24 h (29 mEq/24 h). Estimations of total body water and total exchangeable potassium were below normal. Plasma cortisols were normal.

1. What is the most likely diagnosis?
2. Give two other possible causes for the electrolyte abnormalities present in this case.
3. What further investigations would confirm your most likely diagnosis?
4. What treatment may reverse the electrolyte abnormalities present?

This boy has muscle weakness, a normal blood pressure, hypokalaemia, increased serum bicarbonate concentration, and raised plasma renin activity.

Hypokalaemia may be associated with gastrointestinal loss of potassium (e.g. repeated vomiting, diarrhoea or purgative abuse), renal loss of potassium (DIURETIC THERAPY OR ABUSE, licorice ingestion or therapy with carbenoxolone, and HYPERALDOSTERONISM, primary or SECONDARY). Other causes include anorexia nervosa, diabetes insipidus and pyelonephritis.

In this case the normal blood pressure and high renin exclude primary hyperaldosteronism and other causes of mineralocorticoid excess. The 'normal' renal potassium excretion in the face of a low plasma potassium suggest inappropriate loss of potassium by the kidneys, and abuse of diuretics, e.g. thiazides could produce this picture, with stimulation of the renin-angiotensin-aldosterone system. Ingestion of sodium-retaining agents, e.g. licorice, would not be associated with low total body water, nor of elevated plasma renin levels.

This clinical presentation is that of BARTTER'S SYNDROME. The underlying abnormality is an intrarenal defect in sodium metabolism characterised by a reduced renotubular reabsorption of sodium leading to an increased fraction of filtered sodium being presented to the distal nephron where potassium is secreted. Thus, a greater fraction than normal of sodium and potassium is excreted in the urine. There is an increase in the renal synthesis of prostaglandins and this may lead to the hyperreninaemia and hyperaldosteronism. Furthermore a hypo-responsiveness of blood vessels to the pressor effects of angiotensin II can be demonstrated in these patients; thus, despite high levels of renin, the blood pressure does not rise above normal.

The diagnosis may be supported by RENAL BIOPSY where hyperplasia of the juxtaglomerular apparatus is characteristically seen; REDUCED PRESSOR RESPONSES TO INFUSED ANGIOTENSIN II; and INCREASED URINARY PROSTAGLANDIN EXCRETION.

Reversal of the clinical, electrolyte and other biochemical abnormalities in this syndrome occurs rapidly after treatment with PROSTAGLANDIN SYNTHESIS INHIBITORS, e.g. Indomethacin.

Case 34

A 47-year-old woman was admitted to hospital with a two day history of pain in the chest radiating down both arms. The pain was brought on initially by carrying heavy shopping bags, and was associated with shortness of breath, sweating and palpitations. On one occasion she vomited a small volume of unremarkable fluid. Apart from generalised weakness she had no other symptoms.

26 years previously she had had 'pleurisy' and was hospitalised for a year. No further details were available for this illness. Ten years ago she was diagnosed as having myasthenia gravis. Routine investigations at this time revealed a small thymoma, but surgery was not undertaken and the patient had been adequately controlled with anticholinesterases until the present admission.

Examination at the time of admission revealed a myasthenic facies and a pyrexia of 37.5°C. There was no cyanosis. There was a tachycardia of 140 per minute, sinus rhythm, poor volume. The blood pressure was 90/60 mmHg, the JVP elevated to the angle of the jaw, and the apex beat was not palpable. The heart sounds were very faint, no murmurs were present. Chest expansion was moderately good. There was dullness to percussion at the left base with no added sounds. The liver was palpable 3 cm below the right costal margin and tender. Bulbar weakness and generalised weakness of the limbs was noted.

Investigations showed: Hb 11.9 g/dl (11.9 g%), WBC 14 × 10⁹/1 (14 000/mm³), ESR 115 mm/h. Urea and electrolytes normal. Chest X-ray showed a uniformly enlarged heart and left pleural effusion. ECG was of low voltage with a sinus tachycardia and depressed ST segments in all limb leads.

1. Give two possible causes for her recent deterioration.
2. How could her previous history account for the cardiac findings?
3. What six further investigations would be most useful?

The initial history of chest pain and dyspnoea brought on by exertion suggests ischaemic heart disease. The information given in the history taken in conjunction with the examination findings provide alternatives. A low cardiac output, grossly elevated venous pressure, an impalpable apex beat and low voltage ECG must suggest a pericardial effusion. Kussmaul's sign is not easily demonstrated with gross elevation of neck veins, but pulsus paradoxus may be present.

From the history it may be that the previous pleuritic illness was TUBER-CULOUS and this suggests a possible cause for the subsequent effusions. However, a THYMOMA was noted ten years previously, and a significant number of tumours of this type undergo MALIGNANT CHANGE. They spread by direct infiltration and invade the pericardium.

Her recent deterioration could, therefore, be due either to ISCHAEMIC HEART DISEASE, or to the development of a PERICARDIAL EFFUSION. Other complications of myasthenia should be considered, such as bronchopneumonia or aspiration pneumonia. These could hardly account for all the physical signs.

Other causes for the pericardial effusion would include collagen diseases, for example SLE, and malignancy (spread from carcinoma of bronchus or oesophagus). Myxoedema is also a rare cause of pericardial effusions.

Further investigations should include CARDIAC ENZYMES, SCREENING OF THE HEART, ECHOCARDIOGRAPHY and a MANTOUX TEST. SPUTUM OR GASTRIC WASHINGS should be obtained for ACID FAST BACILLI, culture and cytology. Examination of blood and serum should include a full blood count, estimations of anti-nuclear antibodies and rheumatoid factor. Finally, PERICARDIAL ASPIRATION AND BIOPSY should be performed, perhaps as a preliminary to thoracotomy.

Case 35

A 37-year-old insurance salesman had been well until the age of 32 when he first noticed mild unsteadiness of gait and altered sensation in the left hand. Two years later a diagnosis of possible multiple sclerosis was made. Symptomatically his condition remained static for five years after which he reported further deterioration in gait, oscillopsia on downgaze, incoordination of both arms and altered sensation first in the left lower limb and then in the right lower limb.

On examination he was noted to have a low cervical hairline. Heel-toe walking was impaired. Romberg's test was positive. There was downbeating nystagmus, and wasting and fasciculation of the left side of the tongue. Both plantar responses were extensor. There was impairment of joint position sensation in the hands more than in the feet and the two point discrimination threshold was 9 mm in all digits of the left hand.

1. What is the localisation of this lesion?
2. Give two differential diagnoses.
3. What radiological investigations are indicated?
4. What investigations might have helped to confirm or exclude a diagnosis of multiple sclerosis when he was 34?

The patient's history and signs are typical of an abnormality at the level of the foramen magnum. The diagnosis was an ARNOLD-CHIARI MALFORMATION with associated CEREBELLAR ECTOPIA (i.e. herniation of the cerebellar tonsils through the foramen magnum). A low hairline is associated with this condition. SYRINGOMYELIA WITH SYRINGOBULBIA alone could produce such a picture, as could CONGENITAL PLATYBASIA or BASILAR INVAGINATION (the latter sometimes secondary to PAGET'S DISEASE). A tumour at the foramen magnum such as a MENINGIOMA, NEUROFIBROMA or CHORDOMA would also be a possibility. Downbeating nystagmus which produces oscillopsia when the patient looks down to read or to go down stairs is classical of lesions at this site. The history and signs are not characteristic of multiple sclerosis.

Radiological investigations should include PLAIN SKULL X-RAYS with views of the skull base, CERVICAL SPINE X-RAYS, MYELOGRAPHY with adequate visualisation of the cerebellar tonsils and craniocervical junction. COMPUTERISED AXIAL TOMOGRAPHIC SCANNING of the posterior fossa and upper cervical cord will demonstrate medulla compression or a syrinx. Vertebral angiography may be necessary to define a tumour circulation if surgery is contemplated.

A diagnosis of multiple sclerosis should have been supported by CSF examination with CYTOLOGY and PROTEIN ELECTROPHORESIS for typical oligoclonal IgG bands. VISUAL EVOKED and BRAINSTEM EVOKED RESPONSES should also have been sought.

The patient underwent surgical decompression of the foramen magnum. The ataxia of gait improved over the next two years, but the nystagmus and oscillopsia remained unaltered and were really quite disabling.

Case 36

A woman of 29, recently married, went to her GP complaining of shortness of breath which had occurred spasmodically over the previous six months. Her attacks of dyspnoea had been worse at night and had not occurred during her summer holiday in Majorca. On examination the GP could find no abnormality and considered the attacks to be 'functional' in origin. However they persisted, and on three occasions a relief doctor had been called to see her at night and had prescribed an inhaler which had relieved her symptoms. When she was referred to a Casualty department two months later, in an acute attack, she was breathless, distressed and on auscultation of the chest widespread rhonchi were audible, most pronounced on expiration. She responded slowly and only after several doses of intravenous aminophylline had been given. On admission to the ward she was started on steroids.

1. Name five physical signs that would help you assess the gravity of her situation?
2. How would your answers to the first question affect your further management of this patient?
3. What factors would suggest an allergic aetiology to her asthma?
4. How would this affect your subsequent management?

Although attacks of breathlessness may well be functional or hysterical in nature, such a diagnosis should be entertained only after eliminating all possible organic causes. The intermittent nature of the episodes and freedom from symptoms between attacks strongly suggests asthma. The diagnosis is indeed born out by the findings on her subsequent presentation in casualty.

The danger signs in a patient with asthma include TACHYCARDIA, CYANOSIS, DEHYDRATION, EXHAUSTION, HYPOTENSION, PRONOUNCED PULSUS PARADOXUS and the INABILITY TO EXPECTORATE TENACIOUS SPUTUM.

If necessary, further assessment can be obtained by simple spirometry, the peak flow rate and by the arterial blood gases. Early in the asthmatic attack, hypoxia occurs and the resultant hyperventilation causes hypocapnia. As fatigue sets in, however, hypoventilation ensues and the $PaCO_2$ starts to rise. This is a severe sign and often heralds the need to initiate INTERMITTENT POSITIVE PRESSURE RESPIRATION.

Dehydration necessitates FLUID REPLACEMENT, orally or intravenously, and treatment of the severe case otherwise consists of HIGH DOSE OXYGEN THERAPY (if no chronic obstructive airways disease), BRONCHODILATORS given intravenously and by inhalation, and CORTICOSTEROIDS. Some physicians would routinely give a broad spectrum antibiotic to cover any possible bacterial infective component. If ventilation is undertaken, then bronchial lavage can be performed to remove sputum plugs, although its efficacy is unproven.

Evidence of an allergic aetiology should be sought from a past HISTORY (and possibly family history) of ATOPIC DISEASES. Besides asthma, these include eczema, hay fever and allergic rhinitis. It is important to take a detailed history of the attacks with respect to any possible ALLERGENS (such as house dust mite or animal danders). Atopic individuals have HIGH LEVELS OF CIRCULATING IgE and specific sensitivity can be shown by SKIN TESTS, RADIOALLERGOSORBENT TESTS (RASTs) and, in a few centres, bronchial challenge tests. Therapeutically, it is important to pin-point specific allergies for the AVOIDANCE of ALLERGENS and the fact that DISODIUM CROMOGLYCATE is more likely to be effective. Desensitisation, although often helpful in children, is of little benefit in adult asthmatics.

Case 37

A woman of 25 went to see her GP as she had developed intermittent fever, muscle pains, listlessness and had felt unwell for three weeks. She was normally well and on no medication. There was no known contact with infectious disease and no recent history of travel abroad.

On examination she was pyrexial (38°C) and had several slightly tender enlarged lymph glands in her neck. The only other abnormal findings were that she had a palpable liver and the spleen tip was also felt. In her left groin she had some enlarged lymph glands. The rest of the examination was normal.

Investigations: Hb 13.0 g/dl (13.0 g%), ESR 40 mm/h, WBC 6 × 10⁹/l (6000/mm³) (50% lymphocytes), platelets 250 × 10⁹/l (250 000/mm³), film showed some abnormal mature monocytes. Liver function tests: aspartate transaminase 80 U/1, bilirubin 17 μ m/1 (1 mg%), alkaline phosphatase 125 U/1, Paul-Bunnell test negative. Chest X-ray normal.

1. Give 5 differential diagnoses.
2. What further investigations would you like?

This young lady has a three week history of a non-specific malaise and is now pyrexial with enlarged lymph glands in her neck and groin, and signs of liver and spleen enlargement. Her investigations show her to have mild hepatic disease and a lymphocytosis which, in view of her history, would point to infectious mononucleosis. However, her Paul-Bunnell is negative, which makes the diagnosis much less likely, although the appearance of heterophil antibody may be delayed.

There are several causes of a syndrome that resembles infectious mononucleosis, but with a negative Paul-Bunnell test. The most common of these are due to infection by CYTOMEGALOVIRUS and TOXOPLASMA GONDII. Cytomegalovirus is diagnosed by serology but care must be taken that the assay does not cross-react with EB virus. Toxoplasmosis is also identified by a rising antibody titre and the dye test is often used. Infectious hepatitis may present in this way, although lymphadenopathy is not usually so marked, and the HBsAg should be assayed.

Bacterial infections must be considered and BRUCELLOSIS can cause this clinical picture. There might be a history of exposure to cattle or goats or of the consumption of possibly infected milk or cheese. The organism can sometimes be isolated from blood culture or again the illness can be diagnosed histologically. Despite the lack of cardiac signs, the importance of the diagnosis means that INFECTIOUS ENDOCARDITIS must be considered and blood cultures taken. Tuberculosis is unlikely in view of the widespread lymphadenopathy and her normal chest X-ray.

Non-infectious causes are possible and she might be suffering from Hodgkin's disease or another LYMPHOMA. If this is considered likely, a gland should be removed for histology and at the same time the opportunity should be taken to send part of the gland for bacterial and AFB culture. A rarer cause of a similar clinical picture, but which can also be associated with abnormal circulating cells, is angioimmunoblastic lymphadenopathy. This lady, however, is rather young.

Although unlikely, her blood picture does not exclude a LEUKAEMIA and a bone marrow biopsy might need to be performed. If the diagnosis is still uncertain a liver biopsy might be diagnostic. Again, fragments of marrow and liver should be sent for culture.

Case 38

A 54-year-old Irish railwayman came home drunk one night, and fell downstairs. His wife left him there until the morning, when he awoke and complained of a bad pain in his back and inability to move his legs. His wife and a friend carried him to bed, where he remained until the next day. As his legs were still immobile, he was sent to hospital.

When he was examined the neurological signs in the legs were: absent reflexes including plantar reflexes, a flaccid paralysis of all movements, absent pain and temperature sensation, but normal touch, vibration and joint position sensation. The absence of pain and temperature sensation extended onto his trunk up to a level corresponding to the T11 dermatome. The bladder was distended and the upper edge was palpated at the level of the umbilicus. He had no control over micturition. General examination showed a regular pulse, rate 96/min. There was difficulty feeling the pulse in the left arm, but it was easy to find on the right. The blood pressure in the left arm was 90/60 mmHg and in the right arm it was 160/110 mmHg. The pulses in the right groin and leg were impalpable. There was blood in the urine on microscopy.

A medical registrar made a diagnosis of polyarteritis nodosa. Soon after the patient reached the ward he complained of an excruciating pain between the shoulder blades, and dropped dead. Resuscitation was unsuccessful, and at necropsy the registrar was proved wrong.

1. Explain the neurological signs.
2. Suggest the correct diagnosis.

The only neurological functions preserved below T11 are touch, vibration and joint position sensation. These run wholly or in part in the dorsal columns of the spinal cord, dorsal to all other spinal cord tracts and neurones – including those mediating other sensations, motor functions, and bladder control – hence all the neurological abnormalities can be explained by a single lesion involving the anterior half of the spinal cord at and below T11. The symptoms were sudden in onset, so a vascular event seems likely. The anterior half to two thirds of the cord is supplied by the anterior spinal artery, so the lesion could be an acute obstruction of the anterior spinal artery.

There is also complete or partial obstruction of arteries in the left arm and right leg, and this picture of scattered arterial obstructions led the registrar to diagnose polyarteritis nodosa. Microscopic haematuria is found in polyarteritis nodosa when there is intrarenal arterial involvement, so this supported the diagnosis. However, the vessels involved in polyarteritis nodosa are usually much smaller than the major limbs arteries, and arteritis involving arteries of large size is very rare and usually presents with gradual rather than acute obstructions: Takayasu's disease is an example. Pain occurred at the start and at the end of this illness, and was at one time very severe.

The correct diagnosis must be of a disease that can progress to sudden death over a few days, intermittently very painful, causing acute obstructions of major arteries to the extent that blood pressure in the two arms can be different. At post mortem, a dissecting aneurysm was found, and is compatible with all these features: the dissection extended from the arch of the aorta near the left subclavian artery to the bifurcation of the aorta and down the right common iliac artery. Haematuria is seen with dissecting aneurysm if the renal arteries are involved, and sudden death follows aortic rupture (as in this case) or retrograde dissection back to the aortic ring and pericardium.

Case 39

A 40-year-old bus conductor was referred for investigation. He was well until three months before admission, when he developed a flu-like illness with myalgia, night sweats and a cough productive of a little yellow sputum. His general practitioner thought he had a viral pneumonia and treated him with a variety of antibiotics and cough linctuses. Four weeks later he developed recurrent episodes of central abdominal pain coming on after food and only partially relieved by antacids. He had never vomited, but on two occasions he had had diarrhoea with some fresh blood in the stool. There was no previous history of note, but he had noticed a recent weight loss of 10 lb.

On examination, he had a temperature of 37.8°C. His blood pressure was 160/90 mmHg, and pulse was 108 per minute. Chest examination showed inspiratory bilateral wheezing. The abdomen was normal, but on sigmoidoscopy he had second degree piles. General examination was otherwise unhelpful.

Investigations: Hb 11.4 g/dl (11.4 g%), WBC 17 × 10^9/l (17 000/mm^3), platelets 380 × 10^9/l (380 000/mm^3), ESR 60 mm/h. Urea and electrolytes, chest X-ray and barium meal were all normal. Bilirubin 16 μmol/l (0.9 mg%), aspartate transaminase 83 U/l, alkaline phosphatase 140 U/l. Sputum culture was sterile. His ECG showed a sinus tachycardia.

1. What is the diagnosis?
2. How would you establish it? Give 6 other useful investigations.

This man has a generalised illness causing respiratory and abdominal symptoms. His yellow sputum was sterile and although this may have been due to antibiotic therapy, a search for SPUTUM EOSINOPHILS should be made. This is particularly relevant in view of his bronchospasm. His abdominal pain is highly suggestive of mesenteric ischaemia and a BARIUM MEAL AND FOLLOW-THROUGH may show 'thumbprinting' of the small bowel due to mucosal oedema. It will also exclude a peptic ulcer and a neoplasm.

The presence of vascular disease and a high ESR suggests a vasculitis, which in a man of this age, suggests POLYARTERITIS NODOSA. A DIFFERENTIAL FULL BLOOD COUNT may show eosinophilia and neutrophilia and in combination with a high ESR is very suggestive. Blood should be examined for HEPATITIS B SURFACE ANTIGEN in view of the abnormal liver function tests and is present in up to 30% of all cases. The absence of ANTI-NUCLEAR ANTIBODIES will exclude systemic lupus erythematosus. Histological evidence of vasculitis with characteristic polymorph infiltrate and fibrinoid around arteries is characteristic. Favoured sites for biopsy are kidney, muscle, testicle or skin nodules. In this case, however, there are no skin lesions, and there are no definite indications for renal biopsy. Muscle biopsy has a low success rate and testicular biopsy, although recommended by some authorities, has yet to gain widespread acceptance. Recently, arteriographic changes have been found to be helpful in the diagnosis of polyarteritis nodosa.

In this patient, SELECTIVE MESENTERIC ANGIOGRAPHY is indicated – the finding of multiple aneurysms of the same and varying size in visceral arteries is almost pathognomonic.

Case 40

A 33-year-old policeman was referred to Outpatients after his GP had found his blood pressure to be 170/115 mmHg at an insurance examination. Physical examination showed no abnormalities apart from tortuosity of the retinal vessels, and investigations revealed no underlying cause for his hypertension. Within four weeks his blood pressure returned to 140/90 mmHg on a diuretic.

He was next seen eight weeks later when the following story was obtained. Five days after the start of a mild flu-like illness, he had noticed slight numbness of the right side of his face, and two days after this he had experienced sudden vertigo and vomited twice. Three days later his vertigo had worsened and he became severely ataxic with a tendency to fall to the right. Over the following week he became unable to walk, and other symptoms included tinnitus and partial deafness on the left side.

On examination, apart from a blood pressure of 170/120 mmHg, abnormal findings were confined to the CNS. The fundi showed tortuosity of vessels with no papilloedema. There was bilateral nystagmus on both lateral and vertical gaze, an absent right corneal reflex and minimal right facial weakness with impaired hearing on the left. There was gross incoordination of the limbs with dysdiadokokinesis. All limb reflexes were brisk. Abdominal reflexes were absent and the plantar responses were equivocal.

1. Give three possible causes for his recent illness.
2. What two investigations are indicated?

Concerning this patient's recent neurological illness, the problem is to decide whether this illness is related to his hypertension or whether it is an unrelated condition.

Considering the former – the stepwise progression of the CNS signs is against a BRAIN STEM HAEMORRHAGE, although a succession of small bleeds from a vascular malformation is a possibility. Multiple emboli could present in this way but there was no obvious source in this patient. THROMBOSIS IN THE VERTEBROBASILAR ARTERIAL SYSTEM would be likely in an older patient and several cases have been reported in younger patients with hypertension or diabetes.

In view of the history of a flu-like illness preceding the neurological episode, a POST VIRAL DEMYELINATION should be considered.

Less likely possibilities include a posterior fossa lesion and of these a CEREBELLAR HAEMANGIOBLASTOMA could account for both hypertension and neurological signs.

Investigations indicated include a LUMBAR PUNCTURE (with examination for cells, protein and immunoglobulin), COMPUTERISED AXIAL TOMOGRAPHY and a VERTEBRAL ARTERIOGRAM.

The diagnosis in this patient was vertebrobasilar artery thrombosis. Apart from hypertension, no other precipitating factors for this early presentation of cerebrovascular disease were found in this patient. Four years later he presented with angina of effort and gross triple vessel atheromatous disease was found on coronary angiography.

Case 41

A 48-year-old woman had been working in an East African mission hospital for three years where she had looked after the physiotherapy and radiology departments where she had worked two afternoons a week. Following an attack of diarrhoea she went to her doctor and was found to have a Hb 8.2 g/dl (8.2 g%), WBC 2.3 × 10⁹/l (2300/mm³) (70% lymphocytes), platelets 60 × 10⁹/l (60 000/mm³). There was no history of drug ingestion in any form. She was not on a contraceptive pill and did not take any malaria prophylaxis. Apart from being pale there were no other abnormal physical signs and a bone marrow biopsy showed a uniform decrease in all elements with fatty replacement; no abnormal cells were seen.

It was felt she should stop working in the radiology department. She continued to be pale and six months later returned to England where she was given unknown quantities of iron, folic acid and vitamin B12. One year after her return to England she was seen in Outpatients where she was found to have Hb 6.2 g/dl (6.2 g%), WBC 1.8 × 10⁹/l (1800/mm³) (lymphocytes 65%), platelets 60 × 10⁹/l (60 000/mm³). A splenic tip was palpable on careful examination but there was no hepatomegaly and no other abnormal signs. Two attempts at sternal marrow biopsy were unsuccessful.

1. What are the three most likely diagnoses?
2. What would be the four most useful investigations?
3. How would you monitor her progress?

The haematological investigations indicate that this patient has an aplastic anaemia and the difficulty here is deciding its aetiology and accounting for her splenomegaly which makes an IDIOPATHIC APLASTIC ANAEMIA unlikely. There is no history of exposure to drugs or toxic chemicals and although RADIATION is a possible cause one might expect it to have a more rapidly fatal course. PAROXYSMAL NOCTURNAL HAEMOGLOBINURIA may present with a pancytopenia and splenomegaly and a history of haemoglobinuria should be sought. Tuberculosis can cause a hypoplastic marrow but with this length of history one would expect to find more constitutional symptoms.

Investigations should include an ILIAC CREST TREPHINE, a BLOOD FILM, HAM'S TEST for acid haemolysis and URINE EXAMINATION FOR HAEMOGLOBIN and haemosiderin.

Patients with aplastic anaemia tend to have a poor prognosis because of infections and haemorrhage. Treatment lies in blood transfusions and attempts to stimulate the bone marrow with androgens such as oxymethalone, the response being monitored by the HAEMOGLOBIN, RETICULOCYTE AND PLATELET COUNTS. Very ocassionally bone marrow transplants have been successful.

Case 42

A 60-year-old man was referred to hospital for investigation of the following symptoms: for the past two years he had noticed progressive difficulty in passing urine and had become impotent. During the last three months he had felt dizzy when rising from his bed in the mornings and also occasionally during the day when getting up from a chair. On four such occasions he had lost consciousness for about one minute.

On physical examination he was noted to have a mild right-sided Parkinsonian tremor of the hand. Examination of the cardiovascular system revealed a regular pulse of 90 beats per minute and a recumbent blood pressure of 180/90 mmHg. There was no cardiomegaly and auscultation of the heart was normal. He was not in cardiac failure. Examination of the respiratory and alimentary systems was normal and the following abnormalities were found on examination of the nervous system: he had evidence of a pseudo-bulbar palsy and bilateral pyramidal signs on examination of the limbs. He had an ataxic gait and further testing showed evidence of bilateral cerebellar disturbance.

1. How may his history of loss of consciousness be related to the neurological disturbances?
2. What is the most likely diagnosis?
3. What further investigations would confirm your answers to questions 1 and 2?

The symptoms of dizziness and loss of consciousness on rising to the upright position are strongly suggestive of ORTHOSTATIC HYPOTENSION. Such symptoms are commonly precipitated by drugs and may occur to some extent with advancing age. However, in this case, the history is strongly suggestive of more widespread autonomic impairment and the finding of abnormal pyramidal tract signs, cerebellar dysfunction and Parkinsonism, are all features of MULTIPLE SYSTEM ATROPHY (SHY-DRAGER SYNDROME).

Tests of autonomic function should include the VALSALVA MANOEUVRE which in this case demonstrated an absence of any overshoot of blood pressure during Phase 4 of the manoeuvre. Also, the cardio-accelerator response (increase in pulse rate during Phase 2) was absent. The influence of carotid massage may show absence of slowing of the cardiac rate in autonomic dysfunction and the vasoconstrictor response to cold is also absent in many patients with efferent lesions of the sympathetic pathway.

Biochemical tests of noradrenaline release from sympathetic nerve endings into plasma usually reveal low-low normal levels of noradrenaline and a failure of the levels to rise with tilt is characteristic of autonomic failure.

Treatment of the orthostatic hypotension is largely unsuccessful and has included mineralocorticoids, the use of pressor drugs and anti-gravity suits. Recent reports of benefit from beta-blocking drugs and prostaglandin synthesis inhibitors have not been confirmed in other studies.

Case 43

A 15-year-old West Indian boy had felt unwell for four days with myalgia, lethargy, vague central abdominal pain and vomiting. Several days later his ankle became tender and he was admitted to hospital. His past medical history contained no similar episodes, but he had had recurrent sore throats.

On examination, his temperature was 38°C, his throat was inflamed, but there was no pus visible. Blood pressure was 115/70 mmHg; pulse rate 100 beats per minute. Examination of the cardiovascular system, chest and central nervous system was normal. Examination of the joints revealed mild swelling of the right elbow and tenderness over the right knee. Abdominal examination showed some tenderness around the umbilicus, but no peritonism. Rectal examination was normal, except that the stool was positive when tested for blood. General examination was normal, apart from a mildly inflamed pharynx.

Investigations: Hb 14.3 g/dl (14.3 g%), WBC 7.4 × 10⁹/l (7400/mm³) (normal differential). Platelets 340 × 10⁹/l (340 000/mm³). The blood film was normal and the Paul-Bunnell test negative. Chest X-ray and urea and electrolytes were normal. Blood and urine cultures were sterile. ESR was 30 mm/h.

His abdominal pain resolved over the next week on conservative management, but routine urine testing two weeks after his admission showed haematuria. The urine was sterile on culture.

1. What is the most likely diagnosis?
2. What disease could present with an identical clinical picture?

A combination of swollen joints, abdominal pain with blood in the stools and haematuria suggests a diagnosis of HENOCH-SCHÖNLEIN PURPURA, a condition in which circulating immune complexes produce widespread damage to vascular endothelium and vasculitis. A maculo-papular rash is often, but not always, present, classically involving the ankles, buttocks and elbows. Other causes of polyarthralgia must be considered, including juvenile rheumatoid arthritis, rheumatic fever (now rare) and the arthritis associated with ulcerative colitis and Crohn's Disease. Serum sickness is most unlikely without a recent history of immunisation or drug ingestion. Infectious mononucleosis is unlikely in view of the normal blood film and negative Paul-Bunnell test. However, other viral infections, e.g. rubella and mumps, can present with an acute polyarthritis. Acute leukaemia is unlikely with a normal blood picture and 'collagen diseases' are rare in this age group. Abdominal pain, joint symptoms and haematuria may all occur in a SICKLE CELL CRISIS. The lack of previous episodes and a normal haemoglobin makes this unlikely, however, and the normal blood film and absence of sickle cells excludes the diagnosis.

In HENOCH-SCHÖNLEIN PURPURA severe complications may result from vasculitis affecting the gut and may lead to haemorrhage, perforation, or intussusception. The renal lesion may vary from a mild focal nephritis (usually presenting as slight or intermittent haematuria) to more severe acute glomerulonephritis with diffuse hypercellularity and crescents (proteinuria and progressive impairment of renal function). The prognosis is worse in adults and this is mainly due to the severity of the renal lesion.

Case 44

A 40-year-old secondhand car dealer came to the casualty department with a severe abdominal pain which had been increasing in intensity for 48 hours. He had had a similar, though less severe, attack six months before after which he had become mildly jaundiced for about three weeks. Although he had been investigated in hospital at the time he had received no specific treatment. As a child he had had rheumatic fever and for the last six years he had been on digoxin after developing atrial fibrillation. He had never needed diuretics and had not been on any other drugs.

On examination at the time of admission he was pale, clammy, sweaty, not clinically anaemic and neither jaundiced nor dyspnoeic. In his cardiovascular system his blood pressure was 80/50 mmHg, his JVP was not raised, his pulse was 80 per minute, fibrillating and thready. He had a mid-diastolic murmur at the apex which was conducted to his left axilla. His abdomen was soft and he had epigastric tenderness. Bowel sounds were present. Rectal examination showed soft normal faeces and no localised tenderness.

He was admitted to hospital and over the next two days he remained clammy, cold and hypotensive and also developed paraesthesiae in his legs. His foot pulses were palpable. During the second day he developed dyspnoea and started to cough up frothy white sputum.

1. What is the most likely diagnosis? Give three other possibilities.
2. What six immediate investigations would you perform on admission?
3. How can you explain the features of the subsequent developments?
4. How would you explain his previous attack of jaundice?

This man, who is having his second attack of severe epigastric pain within 6 months, does not have impressive signs of peritonism but is shocked and hypotensive. The most likely diagnoses are ACUTE PANCREATITIS and CHOLELITHIASIS WITH SEPTICAEMIA. The previous history of jaundice makes these more likely. A MYOCARDIAL INFARCTION might present in this way, but the progressive increasing pain would be unusual. A perforated peptic ulcer would be expected to give more evidence of peritonism especially after 48 hours of pain, and a gastrointestinal bleed severe enough to cause shock would be expected to produce a melaena stool after this delay of time. Bleeding, however, could be retroperitoneal, say from a LEAKING AORTIC ANEURYSM, although this generally produces backache. Anyone with mitral valve disease and atrial fibrillation is prone to systemic embolism. A mesenteric embolus would be expected to give more peritonism and perhaps bloody diarrhoea but a SPLENIC EMBOLUS would cause upper abdominal pain. Infective endocarditis must be considered, but is unlikely to cause pain unless via an embolus.

Immediate investigations must include ERECT AND SUPINE ABDOMINAL X-RAYS for pancreatic calcification, radio-opaque gallstones or the rare likelihood of gas under the diaphragm. An ECG must be done and SERUM AMYLASE and BLOOD CULTURES performed. His biochemical state must be assessed with GLUCOSE, UREA AND ELECTROLYTES and if surgery is possible BLOOD GROUPING AND CROSS-MATCHING should be done.

The diagnosis of acute pancreatitis is supported by his subsequent course of prolonged shock during which he develops paraesthesiae due almost certainly to HYPOCALCAEMIA. PULMONARY OEDEMA develops, caused either by failure of his already diseased heart, by acute tubular necrosis following prolonged hypotension or by injudicious fluid therapy.

The previous attack of jaundice could have been caused by BILIARY DUCT COMPRESSION DUE TO PANCREATIC OEDEMA or to CO-EXISTING GALLSTONES. On his recovery he must have a cholecystogram.

Case 45

A 25-year-old woman with insulin dependent diabetes for 15 years was admitted to hospital in ketoacidotic coma. On recovery, she complained that the sight in both her eyes had been progressively deteriorating for the past six months.

Apart from the abnormalities in both eyes and proteinuria, the physical examination was normal.

1. What further investigations would you perform?
2. What are the three potential causes for her visual problems?

Her diabetes was subsequently controlled on twice daily Actrapid and Rapitard insulin.

3. What alteration in vision would you expect to follow such treatment?
4. What further therapy might be indicated to help her vision?

Progressive deterioration of vision in a young diabetic may result from a number of pathological conditions within the eye, of which the most serious is neovascularisation of the retina (retinitis proliferans). The disease of the small blood vessels is, of course, not confined to the eyes and may involve the glomeruli and give rise to impaired renal function. This girl already has proteinuria and thus assessment of renal function with CREATININE CLEARANCE and 24 HOUR PROTEIN EXCRETION should be performed and this will determine the long-term prognosis of the patient.

Visual failure in diabetes can result from CATARACTS, to which diabetics are more susceptible, or the retinopathy which causes visual loss either by producing MACULAR OEDEMA or a PROLIFERATIVE RETINOPATHY. Background retinopathy does not cause visual loss. Young diabetics occasionally rapidly develop a 'snowflake' cataract, but premature 'senile' types of cataract are more commonly found. There is now good evidence that meticulous control of blood sugar is associated with a slower progression of retinopathy and patients should be encouraged to monitor their own blood sugars, possibly with home glucose meters. There is no doubt that panretinal photocoagulation with either laser or xenon light is of benefit to proliferative retinopathy, but photocoagulation of a maculopathy is of less certain benefit because, although the retinal changes can be reversed, visual improvement does not follow. However, some authorities argue that further deterioration is halted and that in future maculopathies may require much earlier treatment. Pituitary ablation or clofibrate no longer have any place in the treatment of retinopathy. Sophisticated vitreous surgery is increasingly successful in removing vitreous haemorrhages and replacing traction retinal detachments in the late stages of retinitis proliferans.

Following stabilisation of her diabetes, there are osmotic changes in the lens which become LESS MYOPIC and there will be changes in vision. This can take several weeks and spectacles should not be prescribed until the eyes have stabilised. Any remaining loss of visual acuity is likely to be due to lens changes and the retinopathy.

Case 46

A 37-year-old right-handed garage mechanic had become aware of impaired hearing in the left ear when aged 34. At the age of 36 his friends commented that he sometimes walked as though he had been drinking and he himself noted that his gait would become very unsteady after drinking a single pint of ale (much reducing his capacity for alcohol).

On examination his gait was unsteady and he tended to veer to the left. Romberg's test was positive. There was a coarse, large amplitude, poorly sustained, first degree nystagmus on left lateral gaze and a finer, smaller amplitude first degree nystagmus to the right. Facial sensation was normal, the right corneal reflex was brisk, the left diminished and there was some weakness of the left facial muscles. Hearing was normal on the right, but he was unable to hear a watch tick at 1 foot on the left. Weber's test (using a tuning fork at 512 Hz) was lateralised to the right. With Rinne's test: right AC >BC, left BC >AC. There was mild incoordination of the left upper and lower limbs. The left plantar response was flexor, the right extensor.

1. What is the site of the lesion?
2. Give at least two causes.
3. How do you explain the results of the tuning fork test?
4. What would you expect caloric tests to show?
5. What investigations are indicated?

The presentation is that of a CEREBELLO-PONTINE ANGLE LESION. Tumours arising at this site include a meningioma, dermoid, epidermoid, metastasis, angioma or glomus tumour. An intrinsic brainstem lesion such as a glioma is unlikely in the absence of other cranial nerve signs. The most likely diagnosis in this patient is a LEFT ACOUSTIC NEUROMA extending extracanalicularly and into the posterior fossa. These usually arise from the inferior branch of the vestibular division of the VIIIth nerve and a common finding on caloric testing is an IPSILATERAL CANAL PARESIS.

Pure tone audiometry showed that the patient was completely deaf in the left ear. The Rinne test result is known as a FALSE POSITIVE as on testing BC the patient actually hears the tuning fork with the opposite ear. The coarse nystagmus to the side of the lesion is a gaze paretic nystagmus indicating disruption of vestibulo-cerebellar connections, the fine nystagmus to the right is gaze evoked nystagmus indicating cross compression of the brainstem vestibular nuclei.

Investigations should include PLAIN SKULL X-RAYS with views of the INTERNAL AUDITORY MEATI, AUDIOMETRY, caloric testing and brainstem evoked potentials. CT SCAN with contrast enhancement with views of the porus is necessary. Other possible tests include vertebral angiography, posterior fossa myelography and metrizamide cisternography and the patient should be examined for cutaneous evidence of neurofibromatosis.

Case 47

A 20-year-old girl student went to see her college doctor after returning from her Easter holiday. She had a three day history of fever, sweats, and muscle pain, and in the last 24 hours had developed ulceration of her tongue and mouth and a very sore throat.

Three weeks before this illness she had been in Turkey on holiday and had been prescribed pain killers by a local doctor. There was no past medical history of serious illness.

On examination she was pyrexial (38.5°C), sweaty and dehydrated. She had oral ulceration and enlarged lymph glands in her neck. The rest of the examination was normal.

Investigations showed a Hb of 13.0 g/dl (13 g%); WBC 1.5×10^9/l (1500/mm³); platelets 200×10^9/l (200 000/mm³); Paul-Bunnell was negative; bilirubin 6.8 μmol/l (0.4 mg%), aspartate transaminase 15 U/l, alkaline phosphatase 95 u/l.

1. What is the most likely diagnosis? Give one other possibility.
2. What investigations should be performed. Give five.

This woman has an acute illness associated with leukopenia. Her leukopenia is most likely to be due to neutropenia and only a few disease processes cause severe neutropenia giving rise to symptoms; these are, DRUG-INDUCED NEUTROPENIA, IDIOPATHIC CHRONIC NEUTROPENIA, ACUTE ALEUKAEMIC LEUKAEMIA and APLASTIC ANAEMIA. A drug-induced neutropenia would be the most common cause of this picture and she has been treated with an analgesic in Turkey. In that country, Amidopyrone, which has been banned in Great Britain, is used as an analgesic and is a well-recognised cause of agranulocytosis. Other drugs which may cause this could include thiouracils and phenylbutazone. Even in the absence of a palpable spleen and no fall in haemoglobin or platelet count, ACUTE LEUKAEMIA must be considered. She does not have the history of a chronic infection, which is often the hallmark of idiopathic chronic neutropenia. Infectious mononucleosis can give this picture rarely, but she has a negative Paul-Bunnell and other unusual causes are viral infections such as influenza or atypical viral pneumonia or brucellosis, but the degree of neutropenia in these cases rarely cause symptoms.

Leukaemia has to be excluded and investigations should therefore include a BLOOD FILM and MARROW EXAMINATION. BLOOD CULTURES should also be done to exclude an associated septicaemia. THROAT SWABS and ULCER SCRAPINGS are necessary to isolate pyogenic organisms and fungi from the lesions in her mouth.

Treatment must be aimed at the primary cause, secondary infection and the prevention of further infection. She must have bacteriocidal antibiotics, she must be barrier-nursed and steroids are used frequently, though there is no evidence that they aid recovery and, indeed, may be dangerous in septicaemia. Any drug which could possibly cause this reaction should obviously be stopped.

Case 48

A 43-year-old traffic warden attended the Outpatient Clinic with a history of pain in the legs. This had come on gradually, starting two years ago, and had progressed to the extent that it was interfering with his job. After walking for 30 minutes, he developed pains radiating down the front of the thigh to the knee and which were relieved by resting. Just before he had to stop, his feet would become 'tired', his legs stiff and he might trip. He smoked 40 cigarettes a day. There was no relevant past history and he was on no medication.

On examination, his blood pressure was 160/110 mmHg. Examination of the cardiovascular system, abdomen, chest, central nervous system and joints was normal. All peripheral pulses were palpable.

Full blood count, ESR and X-rays of both hips were normal.

1. What is the diagnosis?
2. What is the definitive investigation?

The patient gives a classical history of CLAUDICATION OF THE SPINAL CORD. This condition is much underdiagnosed and patients are often thought to have peripheral vascular disease. This is extremely unlikely in this case with normal peripheral pulses. Physical examination is often normal, but on exercise the patient may develop a spastic gait, pyramidal weakness in a leg or an extensor plantar.

Investigations should include a lateral X-ray of the lumbar spine, which may demonstrate a decreased transverse diameter of the spinal canal, i.e. canal stenosis. The most important investigation, however, is a MYELOGRAM which may demonstrate a prolapsed disc, canal stenosis, or, more rarely, a spinal angioma. The latter will appear as a serpiginous structure on the surface of the cord. Should this be the case, further investigation with selective arteriography will demonstrate the exact vascular anatomy prior to excision. Surgery, however, is not usually undertaken in the absence of fixed neurological deficit.

The condition is important to diagnose, as laminectomy may completely cure the symptoms if due to canal stenosis or disc prolapse.

Case 49

A 45-year-old bus conductor, a heavy smoker, had had a constant productive morning cough, and during the previous two years had spent six weeks in hospital after two bouts of influenza.

For one week he had felt unwell and two days prior to admission he had become more dyspnoeic and had complained of inspiratory pain on the right side of his chest.

This time he was centrally cyanosed, febrile and dyspnoeic. The JVP was raised and the liver tender and 5 cm enlarged. His ankles were swollen. The second heart sound was loud in the pulmonary area.

1. Suggest four likely precipitating causes for his present illness.
2. What are the four most useful investigations?

On this admission the patient was in cor pulmonale secondary to chronic lung disease. The second heart sound is produced by the closure of the aortic and then the pulmonary valves and normally the interval between these increases on inspiration. With pulmonary hypertension from the chronic lung disease, the artery pressure is raised and the splitting is narrower with a loud pulmonary second sound.

An ACUTE RESPIRATORY INFECTION, which by exacerbating his hypoxia and consequently his pulmonary vasoconstriction, is the most likely predisposing factor of his heart failure. However, a PULMONARY EMBOLUS or MYOCARDIAL INFARCT must be considered. Patients with obstructive lung disease sometimes rupture an emphysematous bulla producing a PNEUMOTHORAX, and BRONCHIAL CARCINOMA must always be considered in a heavy smoker.

CHEST X-RAY, ECG and SPUTUM CULTURE and CARDIAC ENZYMES are required. A pneumothorax may be diagnosed clinically.

The patient had an acute bronchitis caused by a pneumococcus which responded to antibiotics, low concentrations of oxygen and physiotherapy. He was advised to be immunised against influenza each winter and to start broad spectrum antibiotics as soon as his sputum became purulent.

Case 50

A 24-year-old bus driver came up to the dermatology Outpatients with a 6 week history of itchy spots on his buttocks, elbows, knees and back, which had come up in crops. Apart from these spots he was quite well and there was no relevant medical history. He was not taking any drugs.

On examination he was apyrexial, he had groups of excoriated lesions on his knees, elbows, buttocks and over his right scapula. There were a few intact blisters with surrounding erythema. Examination was otherwise normal.

Initial investigations showed Hb 12 g/dl (12 g%), WBC 7×10^9/l (7000/mm³), film showed macrocytosis, Howell-Jolly bodies and target cells.

1. What do you think the diagnosis is?
2. Suggest two other possible causes of the skin lesions.
3. How do you explain the blood film?
4. What treatment would you give?

This young man has a disease causing grouped itchy bullous lesions which have not affected his mucous membranes, and these are typical of DERMATITIS HERPETIFORMIS. PEMPHIGUS, though a rare disease, does occur in this age group and affects the face, mucous membranes and trunk. It is usually not itchy. Pemphigoid usually affects the over 60 age group and only rarely itches. Other conditions which must be differentiated include PAPULAR URTICARIA, SCABIES and some forms of ECZEMA.

Many would now consider that the presence of IgA deposits at the dermal-papillary junction, demonstrable by immunofluorescence, is a necessary condition for diagnosis. In the past, the rapid therapeutic response to Dapsone was considered diagnostic, but it now appears that other conditions with a similar clinical picture to dermatitis herpetiformis may also respond to Dapsone. There is a strong association of the disease with both HLA B8 and DW3, although this can obviously not be used as a diagnostic test.

Patients with dermatitis herpetiformis, like those with coeliac disease, may develop a gluten sensitive enteropathy with malabsorption and also splenic atrophy. There is a quite high incidence of folate deficiency and megaloblastic changes. Howell-Jolly bodies and target cells are a reflection of the SPLENIC ATROPHY.

Treatment of the disease is with DAPSONE, which has a rapid and profound effect on the lesions. Any associated deficiency due to malabsorption must also be corrected. In addition, patients should be tried on a GLUTEN FREE DIET, which appears to both improve the enteropathy and, in many cases, to enable a reduction in the effective dose of Dapsone. In some cases it has proved possible to stop Dapsone therapy altogether after the initiation of a gluten free diet, with no recurrence of the skin lesions. It may take some months before the gluten free diet shows benefit. Possible toxicity, principally haemolysis, means the lowest effective dose should be used.

Case 51

A 30-year-old man was brought into hospital in an emergency. His friends said that two years previously he had been treated for thyroid trouble with tablets but had not bothered to take these for several months, during which time he had become progressively less well, tired, irritable and short of breath. He smoked at least 30 cigarettes a day, and had stopped working two months previously. Two days before admission he had started to cough up blood and greenish sputum and his condition had deteriorated dramatically; he was now too short of breath to get out of bed.

On examination the man was febrile and obviously very ill. He was drowsy and when roused thought that 'the doctor was the devil come to bury him alive'. He was dirty and unkempt with a marked tremor of his hands and wasting of his body. There was a large pulsating goitre with a systolic thrill and bruit. The pulse was 210 per minute and irregular. His blood pressure was 90/60 mmHg and he had signs of marked cardiac failure and cyanosis. Both eyes were severely proptosed and chemotic but showed no corneal staining with fluorescein.

Whilst in hospital over the next week, he developed deterioration in visual acuity.

1. What drugs would you use to control immediately this man's thyroid state?
2. What other drugs and supportive measures are indicated?
3. Give two possible causes and their treatment for his deterioration in visual acuity.
4. What is the long-term treatment of choice?

This man is an uncontrolled thyrotoxic, now in a state of thyroid crisis probably precipitated by a chest infection. Thyroid crises carry a 20% mortality even with immediate and strenuous treatment.

The objectives of treatment in the short-term are to inhibit further synthesis of thyroid hormones and to antagonise their peripheral effects, to treat any underlying precipitating cause and generally to support the patient.

Further synthesis of thyroid hormones can be rapidly blocked by the administration of IODIDE (10 mg four hourly orally). CARBIMAZOLE (10 mg q.d.s.) should be used in combination as the effect of iodide is often lost after ten days. Treatment of peripheral thyroid hormone effects with propranolol should not be started until the heart failure has been controlled. His precipitating chest infection should be vigorously treated with ANTIBIOTICS after obtaining sputum and blood for culture. Thyrotoxic cardiac failure with atrial fibrillation will respond slowly to DIGOXIN and DIURETICS, but marked improvement will start when thyroid hormones are lowered to normal. General supportive measures are very important; these patients are hyperpyrexial and require vigorous cooling and soluble ASPIRIN. Dehydration is often a problem and intravenous fluids with calories may be needed, and HYDROCORTISONE is often given, as they are shocked.

Deteriorating vision could be explained either by the development of EXPOSURE KERATOPATHY or proptosis causing traction ischaemia or compression of the optic nerve from muscle infiltration. The involvement of extraocular muscles usually produces diplopia rather than visual loss. Treatment for exposure keratopathy initially should include METHYLCELLULOSE EYEDROPS and GUANETHIDINE EYEDROPS and TARSORRHAPHY may well be required. Visual loss from proptosis is an indication for high dose corticosteroids and immunosuppressives, and if there is continued deterioration, surgical decompression of the orbit should be carried out. VERs are useful to monitor visual function.

The alternative long-term treatments in this patient are medical treatment, radioactive iodine or surgery. He is a fickle person, having already failed to take his medication and so the choice lies between thyroidectomy or a therapeutic dose of radioactive ^{131}I.

Case 52

A young woman of 25 presented to her GP with galactorrhoea which had been present for six months. One year ago she had been admitted to a mental hospital with a nervous breakdown and had remained in this establishment for three months. She had regular menstruation and was taking the oral contraceptive pill.

1. Give three possible diagnoses.
2. Give four important investigations.

This woman has galactorrhoea which is most probably associated with hyperprolactinaemia. A raised serum prolactin may be caused by a PROLACTINOMA in the pituitary gland or brought about by DRUG THERAPY or associated with MYXOEDEMA. She has recently been in a mental institution where she may well have received phenothiazines, which can cause hyperprolactinaemia. She is also on the oral contraceptive pill, which is a recognised cause of hyperprolactinaemia and galactorrhoea. Most patients with hyperprolactinaemia have amenorrhoea, but she is on the oral contraceptive pill and having regular withdrawal bleeds.

Investigation must include the measurement of a SERUM PROLACTIN. It is important to exclude a prolactinoma; these are usually microadenomata, but further investigation to exclude a pituitary fossa expanding lesion must include LATERAL SKULL X-RAY and pituitary TOMOGRAPHY, a COMPUTERISED AXIAL TOMOGRAPHIC SCAN and assessment of VISUAL FIELDS. Her THYROID FUNCTION should also be measured. If there is no evidence of a pituitary adenoma, a first step would be to take her off the oral contraceptive pill and also any other drugs which cause raised prolactin levels. If this did not bring about a drop in her prolactin level and a cessation of galactorrhoea, treatment with bromocriptine for a pituitary microadenoma should be considered. Visual field changes would be an indication for pituitary surgery (transsphenoidal) which would also have to be considered with an expanded pituitary fossa.

Case 53

A 72-year-old woman was admitted as an emergency after her family doctor had found her collapsed at home. He had been treating her for a virus infection for the previous six days, during which she had been feeling weak and lethargic with shortness of breath and a cough.

On examination she was semiconscious, confused and dehydrated. She had atrial fibrillation with an apex rate of 140 per minute, blood pressure 130/95 mm Hg. There was no focal neurological signs.

Investigations showed: Hb 16 g/dl (16 gm%); WBC 12 × 10^9/l (12 000/mm³); blood urea 16.6 mmol/l (100 mg%); plasma sodium 150 mmol/l (150 mEq/l); potassium 5.5 mmol/l (5.5 mEq/l); chloride 97 mmol/l (97 mEq/l); bicarbonate 22 mmol/l (22 mEq/l); blood sugar 65 mmol/l (1390 mg%); urine sugar 2%.

1. What is the cause of this patient's collapse?
2. What five further investigations are indicated?
3. Suggest five important steps in treating this patient.

This patient has profound hyperglycaemia and dehydration, but is not acidotic. She therefore presents with HYPEROSMOLAR, NONKETOTIC DIABETIC COMA. This condition has a high mortality and is often associated with late onset diabetes or, alternatively, it may be the presenting feature of the disease. Characteristically, severe hyperglycaemia is associated with dehydration, hypernatraemia, and hyperosmolality of plasma. Although ketoacidosis is not usually found, hyperosmolality and ketoacidosis may coexist. However, investigations should include BLOOD GASES to determine acid-base status. In this patient who presents with a cardiac arrhythmia, an ECG, CHEST X-RAY and CARDIAC ENZYMES would be mandatory. Investigations for a precipitating underlying infection should be sought and should include SPUTUM, BLOOD and MSU CULTURE.

Treatment of this type of diabetic coma requires REHYDRATION and the administration of INSULIN. HYPOTONIC (N/2) SALINE is often used initially and short-acting insulin by a constant infusion, often with smaller doses than required for ketoacidotic states, will reverse the metabolic abnormality. Frequent estimation of BLOOD SUGAR and ELECTROLYTES are essential and intravenous therapy and insulin infusion should be adjusted according to these results.

DIGITALISATION for atrial fibrillation would also be indicated and BROAD-SPECTRUM ANTIBIOTICS should be started after obtaining the specimens for culture.

Hyperosmolar coma causes increased blood viscosity and prophylactic anticoagulation with heparin is advisable.

Case 54

A 27-year-old labourer was admitted to hospital with an acute right lower lobe pneumonia following an upper respiratory tract infection. Although sputum cultures were sterile (he had received two days treatment with tetracycline before admission), he responded well to benzyl pencillin. His fever settled within 24 hours of admission and his general condition improved. At this time, he was noted to have haematuria on routine urine testing, but urine culture was sterile. Microscopy confirmed haematuria, but there was no pyuria. However, when urine culture was repeated four days later, microscopy was normal with no cells or casts visible. He was discharged from hospital and one month later he was discharged from the Outpatient Clinic as his chest X-ray showed complete resolution of his pneumonia.

Six months later he reattended the clinic with a six day history of haematuria following a flu-like illness, which had started one week earlier. There was no accompanying abdominal pain or dysuria. There was no other significant past medical history.

On examination, no abnormalities were found. His blood pressure was 120/75 mm Hg.

The patient was admitted at once for investigation. Full blood count, urea and electrolytes, calcium, liver function tests and clotting screen were all normal. Chest X-ray and IVP showed no abnormality. MSU showed RBCs + +, but no casts and was sterile on culture. Cystoscopy was normal.

1. What is the diagnosis?
2. How would you confirm it?

This patient has had repeated episodes of confirmed haematuria. Cystoscopy and IVP are normal, so the most likely cause of painless haematuria in an otherwise well person is glomerulonephritis. The occurrence of haematuria in association with a febrile illness is very suggestive of BERGER'S DISEASE. It occurs almost always in young or adolescent boys, often associated with an upper respiratory tract infection. Haematuria occurs at the same time or shortly after the upper respiratory symptoms, and may last for several weeks. The haematuria that occurs with acute post-streptococcal glomerulonephritis may occur transiently at the beginning of the illness, but is at its height on about the tenth day. In recent years, post-streptococcal glomerulonephritis has become extremely rare in the United Kingdom. During an acute attack of Berger's Disease, there may be transient impairment of renal function, but there is no fluid retention and the patients remains normotensive. Some patients have persistent proteinuria with or without haematuria. The condition is often benign and transient, but when there are recurrent attacks, the prognosis is less good – some of these patients will develop hypertension and chronic renal failure. Patients under 15 years of age tend to do much better than the older age group, even though they may have recurrent attacks.

The necessary investigation is PERCUTANEOUS RENAL BIOPSY which would show a mild focal and segmental proliferative glomerulonephritis. In contrast with the patchy nephritis, IgA and C_3 are deposited in all the glomeruli.

Case 55

A 46-year-old man was referred to the Outpatient Department complaining of a dull aching pain in the right hypochondrium that had been present for the last two months. He had, however, been feeling generally weak and lethargic for the last year and had lost one stone in weight. On further questioning, he admitted to impotence for six months and said he had decreased his frequency of shaving over this time. He did not smoke and drank two pints of beer on a Saturday night. In his past medical history he had suffered from arthritis in both knees for the last five years but was otherwise well. His only medication was an occasional paracetamol for this arthritis.

On examination, he looked well, being sun-tanned after a recent holiday in Greece. He was not anaemic, jaundiced, cyanosed or clubbed and there was no lymphadenopathy. Pulse 84 per minute, regular with ectopics. JVP + 4 cm. Cardiac apex in the anterior axillary line. He had a prominent third heart sound but there were no murmurs. Chest clinically clear. In the abdomen, the liver was palpable 3 cm below the costal margin, smooth and firm, and the spleen could just be tipped. He had bilateral testicular atrophy and there was crepitus in both knees. Urinalysis negative.

1. What is the most likely diagnosis?
2. How would you confirm this?

This man presents with rather non-specific symptoms of lethargy, weight loss and an abdominal ache. In addition, however, he has signs of cardiac failure with a displaced apex beat, mildly raised venous pressure and a third heart sound. This, in the absence of any valvular lesion, would raise the possibility of a cardiomyopathy. He also has testicular atrophy and hepatosplenomegaly and these, with his heart disease, suggest the diagnosis of HAEMOCHROMATOSIS. He may well also be pigmented, this being confused with or hidden by his sun-tan and, in addition, his arthritis might be related, perhaps through chondrocalcinosis. Although his urinalysis is negative, this does not exclude mild diabetes that should be looked for.

Secondary causes of haemochromatosis should be excluded. These include anaemia with ineffective erythropoiesis (e.g. sideroblastic anaemia), alcoholic cirrhosis and a high oral iron intake. These appear unlikely in this man who probably has IDIOPATHIC HAEMOCHROMATOSIS and a positive family history should be looked for.

Diagnosis is confirmed biochemically and histologically. The SERUM CONCENTRATIONS OF IRON AND FERRITIN are usually raised as is the PERCENTAGE SATURATION OF TRANSFERRIN. The DESFERRIOXAMINE TEST can be used to confirm the presence of parenchymal iron overload. The 24 hour urine secretion of iron is raised following intramuscular desferrioxamine. LIVER BIOPSY is considered the most reliable criterion for the evaluation of both parenchymal iron overload and tissue damage. All first-degree relatives over the age of 10 years should be screened biochemically for iron overload. This should be repeated at regular intervals. In most families the disease is inherited as an autosomal recessive trait.

Case 56

A 57-year-old lorry driver was admitted at the request of his general practitioner. He was normally well apart from his usual morning cough and white sputum, which he attributed to smoking 30 cigarettes a day. Two days before admission his sputum had increased and turned green and he had become increasingly lethargic and breathless. He was on no medication and drank two pints of beer a day.

On examination, he was febrile, dyspnoeic and cyanosed but not clubbed. His tongue was dry. Pulse 130/minute and regular; blood pressure 130/80 mmHg Auscultation of his chest revealed an area of bronchial breathing together with a few crackles at the left base. He had a fine tremor, his reflexes were brisk and there were no focal neurological signs.

Investigations: Hb 14.2 g/dl (14.2 g%), WBC 24 × 10⁹/l (24 000/mm³) (95% neutrophils); ESR 70 mm/h, sodium 132 mmol/l (132 mEq/l, potassium 3.6 mmol/l (3.6 mEq/l), urea 4.0 mmol/l (24 mg%), glucose 5.0 mmol/l (90 mg%). Aspartate transaminase 30 U/l, bilirubin 13 μ mol/l (0.76 mg%), protein 65 g/l (6.5 g%), albumin 40 g/l (4.0 g%), alkaline phosphatase 105 U/l, calcium 2.25 mmol/l (9.0 mg%), phosphate 0.8 mmol/l (2.5 mg%). Chest X-ray showed left lower lobe consolidation. Sputum microscopy showed gram positive cocci, non acid fast bacilli seen. Urinalysis negative.

A diagnosis of lobar pneumonia was made and he was started on ampicillin. In view of the possible dehydration an intravenous infusion was started and he was given Dextrose saline, 1 litre every four hours. Next day he was markedly improved, his fever was settling and he was less dyspnoeic. The following day, however, he complained of headache and nausea and later vomited his lunch. In the afternoon, he had become increasingly drowsy and confused.

On examination he was afebrile, pulse 100 per minute, blood pressure 140/85 mm Hg, JVP not raised. There were crepitations at the left base. He had no neck stiffness, the pupils were equal and reacted to light and the fundi were normal. He had a generalised increase in muscle tone but no focal neurological signs could be demonstrated.

Investigations: Hb 14.0 g/dl (14.0 g%), WBC 15 × 10⁹/l (15 000/mm³), sodium 115 mmol/l (115 mEq/l), potassium 3.0 mmol/l (3.0 mEq/l), urea 2.5 m/l (15 mg%), pO₂ 10.6 kPa (80 mmHg), pCO₂ 5.6 kPa (42 mmHg). CSF was clear and contained 1 lymphocyte/mm³.

1. What is the most likely diagnosis, and how would you confirm it?
2. How would you treat this?
3. What further investigations would you like to perform?

This man presents with a typical lobar pneumonia that responds well to antibiotics. His mental deterioration is associated with no focal neurological signs and no evidence of meningism. He is well oxygenated and the striking abnormality is his hyponatraemia. With his clinical state and fluid management he is unlikely to be sodium depleted and so water intoxication is probable. He has been given a considerable quantity of intravenous fluid since admission, but his renal function is good and his electrolyte imbalance is unlikely to be due to this alone. It is likely, then, that he is suffering from the syndrome of INAPPROPRIATE SECRETION OF ANTIDIURETIC HORMONE. To confirm this, plasma and urine osmolalities should be determined. The plasma osmolality will be low, but the kidney will not be producing an appropriately dilute urine so its osmolality will be higher than expected.

Treatment consists of FLUID RESTRICTION, a daily input of, say, 500 ml, to allow the body to lose its excess water. Giving saline usually results in its being rapidly excreted in the urine, but plasma sodium may be raised by causing a diuresis with frusemide and infusing 2N saline.

Although inappropriate ADH secretion can occur as a response to a chest infection, it is much more common a manifestation of an oat-cell bronchogenic carcinoma. This man must be further investigated with SPUTUM CYTOLOGY and, if necessary, following his recovery, by BRONCHOSCOPY.

If long-term treatment for inappropriate ADH secretion is necessary, fluid restriction is unpleasant for the patient and demeclocycline or lithium have been used which appear to decrease the renal response to ADH.

Case 57

A 33-year-old Russian engineer, who spent several months each year laying pipelines in Ethiopia, developed a flu-like illness one week after returning to the United Kingdom. This was of abrupt onset and consisted of malaise, headaches, myalgia, vomiting and upper abdominal discomfort. Physical examination revealed a fever of 39.5°C, slight icterus and some tenderness in the right hypochondrium. Urinalysis showed + + protein, + blood and the presence of bile.

Investigations showed: Hb 13.0 g/dl (13.0 g%), WBC 6.0 × 10⁹/l (6000/mm³), ESR 90 mm/h, aspartate transaminase 154 U/l, MSU showed 15–20 red blood cells per high powered field, but was otherwise normal. Stool and blood cultures negative, Brucella agglutinins, Widal and Paul-Bunnell tests all negative. The WR was positive and the chest X-ray normal.

No diagnosis was made and after four days he was treated empirically with ampicillin. His symptoms soon subsided but one week later he relapsed with identical complaints. His liver edge was just palpable, but physical examination was otherwise unchanged.

1. Give three likely diagnoses for this man's illness.
2. Suggest five further investigations.

This man, recently returned from East Africa, has a relapsing febrile illness, with evidence of hepatic and renal involvement. MALARIA must be considered a strong possibility as the episodes of fever in this disease are not always regular, especially with falciparum malaria or a mixed infection. LEPTOSPIROSIS can cause a similar picture; although patients usually get a leucocytosis, the white count is often initially low. Penicillin only affects the course of this disease if given very early. RELAPSING FEVER (either tick- or louse-borne) might well present this way and penicillin does not prevent the relapses. Like the above diagnoses, it often has an abrupt onset. YELLOW FEVER is less likely; it could easily have caused his initial illness and there may be an episode when fever remits, although this seldom lasts as long as a week. Other viral infections (hepatitis, Dengue or haemorrhagic fevers) would be unlikely in view of the relapsing nature of the disease, and they are usually insidious in onset. Schistosomiasis is also an unlikely possibility, although there may be an episode of fever (with S. mansoni and not S. haematobium) some weeks after infection. Non-infective causes are also possible such as polyarteritis nodosa or a renal cell carcinoma with liver involvement.

Further investigations include the examination of THICK or THIN BLOOD FILMS for malarial parasites and Borrelia spirochaetes. In addition, Leptospira spirochaetes may be seen, but they are difficult to recognise. Leptospira is usually grown from the blood early in the illness (and his negative culture makes the diagnosis less likely). Later in the illness the organism may be grown from urine and repeat URINE CULTURE is necessary. Blood must also be sent for detection of LEPTOSPIRA ANTIBODIES by agglutination or complement fixation tests. YELLOW FEVER ANTIBODIES must also be sought, but as they remain in high titre after an infection, it is necessary to demonstrate a rising titre. Blood should also be sent for HBsAg determination. S. mansoni would be diagnosed by finding OVA in STOOLS OR RECTAL BIOPSY; serological methods are poor. Finally, if no cause has been found for this man's haematuria, an IVP and cystoscopy should be performed.

False positive WRs are common with any spirochaetal disease or with infections such as malaria or glandular fever. It may occur with autoimmune disease or occasionally after vaccination or any febrile illness. More specific tests such as FLUORESCENT TREPONEMAL ANTIBODY TEST and TREPONEMA PALLDUM IMMOBILIZATION TESTS should be performed.

Case 58

A 48-year-old businessman went to see his doctor soon after returning home from a month's holiday in Sicily with his family. He did not feel any better for the break and had recently complained of vague headaches. Although he took little exercise and smoked and drank to excess he had never been seriously ill. He had recently lost a little weight.

On examination he was tanned. His blood pressure was 170/115 mmHg and, apart from a grade II hypertensive retinopathy, there were no other abnormal signs. The blood biochemistry showed urea 7.1 mmol/l (43 mg%), plasma sodium 147 mmol/l (147 mEq/l), potassium 2.7 mmol/l (2.7 mEq/l), bicarbonate 30 mmol/l (30 mEq/l), pH 7.5.

1. What is the most likely diagnosis?
2. What are two other possible diagnoses?
3. Suggests two tests that would confirm or refute your most likely diagnosis.

Aldosterone enhances sodium and potassium exchange in the distal convoluted tubule thereby causing hypokalaemia, alkalosis and a high urinary potassium excretion. The biochemical picture in this patient could, therefore, be explained by an inappropriate secretion of aldosterone (Conn's syndrome), secondary hyperaldosteronism (less likely in view of the high plasma sodium), or other steroids which have a mineralocorticoid action (Cushing's syndrome). In this patient, especially as he is a heavy smoker, an ACTH SECRETING CARCINOMA OF THE BRONCHUS must be considered. His suntan might not be due solely to his recent holiday as hyperpigmentation is frequently found in extra-adrenal tumours. A chest X-ray must be performed and the diagnosis would be confirmed biochemically by finding raised PLASMA CORTISOLS which would not be suppressed by a DEXAMETHASONE SUPPRESSION TEST. Sputum cytology and possibly bronchoscopy may be indicated.

CONN'S SYNDROME, in which plasma ALDOSTERONE levels are raised, with suppression of PLASMA RENIN ACTIVITY, or CUSHING'S SYNDROME due to adrenal adenoma, adrenal hyperplasia or a pituitary basophil adenoma are less likely statistically, but nevertheless a skull X-ray for evidence of pituitary enlargement is required. Occasionally accelerated hypertension may be accompanied by secondary hyperaldosteronism but in this case one would expect to find a more florid retinopathy. High plasma renin levels may occur in the absence of oedema and control of the hypertension results in disappearance of the secondary hyperaldosteronism. A hypokalaemic alkalosis is also seen with diarrhoea, excessive vomiting and diuretic or carbenoxolone therapy.

In Conn's syndrome the distinction between an adenoma and bilateral hyperplasia may be difficult. Patients with an adenoma tend to have a more severe biochemical disturbance with lower levels of plasma potassium, higher secretion rates of aldosterone and greater suppression of plasma renin activity. An adenoma may be localised by arteriography and/or adrenal venography. The latter may be a difficult procedure and carries the danger of adrenal infarction. Radioisotopic labelling of the tumour with ^{131}I-19-iodocholesterol (or alternative isotopes) may be attempted. In some cases computerised axial tomography will identify a tumour. The definitive management of choice is removal of the tumour at laparotomy. Otherwise the hypertension may be controlled by spironolactone in conjunction with other antihypertensive drugs.

Case 59

A 37-year-old taxi driver was referred because of increasing difficulty in performing his job. He had been in good health all his life and had worked in the present job for nine years. Over the past six weeks, however, he had experienced increasing difficulty finding addresses even in areas he knew well. Despite resorting to a street map he was still often unable to get his bearings and following a number of complaints, he was now in danger of losing his job. His wife said the difficulty had started quite suddenly, but he had attributed this to fatigue and family worries; she was worried that he seemed relatively unconcerned. The symptoms appeared to vary from day to day, but the disability was greater at the time of referral than when the symptoms first appeared. He drank three pints of beer and smoked 15 cigarettes daily.

On examination he looked well. He was right-handed. Blood pressure was 130/84 mm Hg; pulse 86 beats per minute and regular. There was no abnormality of the cardiovascular system, chest or abdomen. In the central nervous system he was alert and his memory, general knowledge and speech were normal, but some of his replies were not really appropriate. Examination of the cranial nerves was normal but neurophthalmic testing showed that whilst his visual fields were full and optic discs normal he could not generate an optic kinetic response to his right side. There was no abnormality of power, sensation, tone of reflexes. Both plantar responses were flexor. The following were normal or negative: blood count, ESR, urea and electrolytes, random blood sugar, serum calcium, liver enzymes, thyroid function tests, VDRL and TPHA. X-rays of the chest and skull were normal.

1. What is the localisation of the lesion?
2. What is the likely cause?
3. Give two further investigations.
4. What visual field defect might you expect to find?

This man has a progressive functional disability involving the performance of a single acquired skill and affecting awareness of spatial relationships. This implies a lesion of the NON-DOMINANT PARIETAL LOBE, in his case probably the right side (since he is right-handed). Parietal lobe symptoms may vary from day to day but in this man the history is essentially progressive. An INTRA-CRANIAL TUMOUR is by far the most likely diagnosis. Unfortunately, 45% of all brain tumours in this age group are astrocytomas and a further 15% are metastases. A subdural haematoma would be considered in an older age group, even if there is no history of head injury, and meningiomas in females.

The non-dominant parietal lobe is necessary for appreciation of body image and orientation in extrapersonal space. When this is involved in a disease process, there may be difficulty in getting around, even in familiar surroundings, and inability to recognise landmarks or faces. With further damage, the patient may neglect his contralateral limbs, forgetting where they are, have difficulty in dressing or allow his limbs to lie in a bizarre position. Even though power may be preserved the affected limb may be ignored. These signs may be accompanied by a left inferior quadrant homonymous hemianopia and abnormal optic kinetic responses (the ability to generate a nystagmus to moving stripes on a drum or tape) are typical of parietal lobe tumours.

The relevant investigations in this patient are: An EEG which may shown non-specific lateralising abnormalities and COMPUTERISED AXIAL TOMOGRAPHIC BRAIN SCAN with enhancement will show a single lesion suggesting a tumour. The shape of the lesion and the pattern of enhancement may indicate the likely pathology. Occasionally, multiple lesions are shown which would tend to support a diagnosis of metastases or granulomatous disease.

Case 60

An elderly Irishman was admitted to Casualty, having been found by the police drunk and lying in a pool of vomit in a gutter. He was conscious, febrile, dyspnoeic, but not cyanosed, with a tachycardia and a blood pressure of 190/130 mmHg. Apart from a bruise on his right temple, the abnormal findings were confined to the chest, where he had coarse crepitations at the right base, a pleural rub and a small area of bronchial breathing. His chest X-ray showed collapse and consolidation of the right lower lobe. Skull X-rays were normal and he was started on ampicillin.

The following day, when he was sober, he said his vision had suddenly gone in both eyes prior to his fall and had caused his collapse and injury to his head. He could still not see clearly and on examination had a left homonymous hemianopia. Otherwise neurological examination was normal.

In spite of the appropriate antibiotics and physiotherapy, his temperature remained high over the next four days. He had purulent sputum and repeated small haemoptyses.

1. What was the cause of the sudden loss of vision in both eyes?
2. Why did he develop a hemianopia?
3. What was the probable cause of his continuing pyrexia?
4. What two investigations are necessary on the fourth day?

The occipital cortex contains the visual areas and receives the majority of its blood supply from the posterior cerebral arteries. This man's hypertension and the sudden onset of blindness suggest a BLOCKAGE OF THE BASILAR ARTERY AT THE ORIGINS OF THE POSTERIOR CEREBRAL VESSELS with subsequent fragmentation of the thrombus and EMBOLISATION TO THE RIGHT POSTERIOR CEREBRAL ARTERY. The only other common cause of sudden loss of vision in both eyes is hysteria. He is unlikely to obtain any more than a marginal improvement in his hemianopia, but as the macula is spared, he will still have normal visual acuity.

It is easy to be misled and dismiss a patient smelling of alcohol as simply to be drunk and not to have any other pathology. However, one must be aware of the occasional pitfalls and this was suggested on the man's admission by the signs of collapse and consolidation in the right lung. Foreign bodies are most commonly aspirated into the right lower lobe bronchus. Drunk patients with a depressed protective cough reflex are more likely to inhale foreign bodies. His chest X-ray confirmed the consolidation, but showed no foreign body. These are frequently radiolucent or have the same radio-density as the mediastinum. If there is any suspicion of an aspirated foreign body TOMOGRAPHY may reveal its presence, but in any case early BRONCHOSCOPY is essential and if found the foreign body can be removed.

A piece of mutton bone was removed with some difficulty from the right lower lobe bronchus. With continued antibiotic therapy and intensive physiotherapy he made a full recovery.

Case 61

A 28-year-old woman journalist went to see her GP as she had been feeling unwell for six weeks with anorexia, lethargy, joint pains and a loss in weight of more than a stone.

On examination she was thin, pale, apyrexial and jaundiced. Her abnormal physical signs were confined to her abdomen, where she had a palpable liver three cm below her right costal margin, and the tip of the spleen was also palpable.

Investigations: Hb 11.0 g/dl (11.0 g%), WBC 6 × 10⁹/l (6000/mm³), bilirubin 34 μmol/l (2 mg%), alkaline phosphatase 140 U/l, aspartate transaminase 800 U/l, albumin 24 g/l (2.4 g%), globulin 53 g/l (5.3 g%).

1. What four further points from her history should be documented?
2. What is the most likely diagnosis?
3. What three further investigations would help you establish a diagnosis?

This young woman has liver disease and her biochemistry suggests hepatocellular damage rather than an obstructive pattern. It is very important to know whether she is a HEAVY DRINKER and also to obtain a DRUG HISTORY for possible toxic compounds. In addition, enquiry should be made about any episodes of PREVIOUS JAUNDICE.

Her clinical picture would fit with a VIRAL HEPATITIS; probably type B in view of the length of symptoms and her arthritis (caused by immune complexes). A history of CONTACT OR RECENT INJECTIONS should be sought.

Her raised globulin, however, suggests that the most likely diagnosis is CHRONIC ACTIVE HEPATITIS. There are several causes of this histological picture and it can occur after hepatitis caused by both type B and non A-non B viruses. In addition, it can be precipitated by drugs or alcohol and rarer causes are Wilson's disease and alpha$_1$-antitrypsin deficiency. A large proportion of cases are of unknown aetiology (but perhaps autoimmune) and these 'lupoid' cases often present in young women.

Necessary investigations include a test for HEPATITIS B SURFACE ANTIGEN which is positive in both the acute infection and those that progress to chronic hepatitis. Serum PROTEIN ELECTROPHORESIS is necessary to define the cause of her hyperglobulinaemia and differential immunoglobulin levels may show the increased IgG that occurs in chronic active hepatitis. SERUM AUTOANTIBODIES should be looked for as in 'lupoid' chronic active hepatitis, anti-smooth muscle antibodies are found in 60% of cases and anti-mitochondrial antibodies in 25%. In addition, anti-nuclear antibody, Wasserman and rheumatoid factors may all be positive. If there is no obvious cause for her liver disease, or if she remains persistently HBsAg positive, then a LIVER BIOPSY should be performed after checking her CLOTTING STUDIES. Chronic active hepatitis of any severity, especially if HBsAg negative, should be treated with steroids, whereas the benign CHRONIC PERSISTENT HEPATITIS (which can give a similar clinical picture) needs no treatment. The value of steroids in HBsAg positive cases is debatable.

Infectious mononucleosis can cause a hepatitis picture, but here the absence of pharyngitis and lymphadenopathy makes it unlikely. Primary biliary cirrhosis is unlikely to cause her biochemistry and she has no itching.

Case 62

A 75-year-old widow presented with a history of deteriorating vision in both eyes for the last three months and because of this she found it difficult to look after herself. She was on no medication and said she was otherwise well, but she recently had several falls resulting in a fracture of the neck of the right femur 18 months previously. This had been repaired surgically and following this she had problems with bedsores. Her falls were not associated with loss of consciousness, fits or vertigo. She had recovered without complication from pulmonary tuberculosis aged 21 years and she smoked 15–20 cigarettes a day.

On examination she was thin and frail and slightly paranoid. She saw 6/60 in each eye. She was unable to read any of the Ishihara colour test plates. The ocular media were clear and the optic discs normal. Visual fields showed bilateral central scotomas to red targets. Ocular examination was otherwise normal. Neurologically, muscle power in her limbs was quite good and tone was normal. She had absent ankle jerks, flexor plantar responses, other reflexes were normal. Joint position sensation was reduced in her feet and vibration could not be appreciated below her knees. Sensation in her arms was normal. Romberg's sign was mildly positive and she had some heel-shin ataxia.

Investigations: Hb 12.1 g/dl (12.1 g%), WBC 7.9 × 10⁹/1 (7900/mm³), ESR 34 mm/h, PCV 41, MCHC 19 mmol/l (30%), MCV 90 fl (90 μ^3), urea and electrolytes normal.

1. Suggest two differential diagnoses.
2. What other information do you require?
3. What four investigations are necessary?

This patient had mild posterior column sensory loss and gross bilateral visual failure. The combination of bilateral poor acuity, colour loss and central scotomas suggest that this is due to optic nerve disease, in spite of the normal appearance of the optic discs. These signs suggest a NUTRITIONAL OR TOXIC AMBLYOPIA as the cause of her problems. Some elderly patients are often vague or fanciful about their diet and it requires persistence to get an ADEQUATE DIETARY HISTORY and details of their tobacco and alcohol consumption and medication. B12 DEFICIENCY is unlikely in view of the blood film, but SERUM LEVELS OF B12 and FOLATE must be measured. Some evidence of poor nutrition might be found in low levels of plasma proteins and the association of pernicious anaemia and gastric carcinomas must be remembered.

Nutritional amblyopia is not uncommon among elderly patients who do not look after themselves and it seems to be due to a combination of factors rather than purely to smoking or pernicious anaemia. The optic discs characteristically look normal. Visual recovery is usually dramatic over a period of weeks on vitamin supplements, B12 and a good diet.

Although the sensory signs would not support a compressive lesion affecting the optic nerves or chiasm as the cause of her visual failure, this must be considered and excluded by SKULL X-RAYS and a CT SCAN. The progressive nature of her symptoms suggests that optic nerve ischaemia is unlikely but occasionally a CARCINOMATOUS OPTIC NEUROPATHY can present like this and if this is considered, CSF must be obtained for cytology and a primary tumour (usually breast or lung) searched for in the normal way. In any patient with a combination of optic nerve disease and posterior column signs, SYPHILIS must be excluded. With modern SEROLOGY (FTA and TPHA) it is most unusual to get a negative blood serology and positive serology in the CSF, but this can occur rarely.

Case 63

A 34-year-old West Indian was admitted to hospital with a complaint of progressive breathlessness over the previous four months. He also had an unproductive cough. He complained that since arriving in England three years before, his hands had become very painful and pale in cold weather.

On examination the abnormal findings were confined to the hands and the chest. In the chest, areas of bronchial breathing and aegophany were noted over the mid zones, with fine crepitations at both bases.

Investigations: Hb, WBC and ESR normal. Chest X-ray showed patchy shadowing in both mid zones and bases, FEV₁ 1200 ml, FVC 1400 ml, arterial blood gases — PaO₂ 8.6 kPa (65 mmHg), PaCO₂ 5.3 kPa (40 mmHg), pH 7.4.

1. What is the most likely diagnosis?
2. What three abnormal findings may have been discovered on examination of the hands?
3. What three further investigations would you perform?

The history of cold intolerance in this patient is strongly suggestive of Raynaud's phenomenon. The primary or idiopathic form of the disease may occur in isolation; however, Raynaud's phenomenon may be associated with several conditions including thromboangitis obliterans, trauma, cervical rib, the collagen diseases, cold agglutinins and cryoglobulinaemia.

The progressive history of breathlessness, together with evidence of a restrictive defect in pulmonary function, associated with hypoxia without hypercapnia, suggests a diffusion abnormality for which there are many possible causes such as fibrosing alveolitis, sarcoid, scleroderma, multiple pulmonary emboli, and so on.

The co-existence of pulmonary disease and Raynaud's phenomenon strongly suggests SCLERODERMA and, in addition to the signs of Raynaud's phenomenon in the hands, SKIN THICKENING with TETHERING OF THE SKIN, SUBCUTANEOUS CALCIFICATION and telangiectasia should be looked for and a history of dysphagia sought.

Further investigations might include measurement of TRANSFER FACTOR (diffusion capacity for carbon monoxide) which would be decreased, a BARIUM SWALLOW for evidence of oesophageal involvement, and a SKIN BIOPSY for histological evidence of scleroderma.

Case 64

A young man of 28 came to his GP with nausea, feeling unwell, nocturnal sweats and weight loss for about a week. He had been discharged from hospital 6 weeks previously where he had been admitted as an emergency with a ruptured spleen following a road traffic accident. He had been on tranquillisers since this accident as his fiancée had been killed in the crash. In his past history he had had a right meniscectomy carried out three years before. On examination he was jaundiced and had cervical lymphadenopathy. His respiratory and cardiovascular systems were normal. In his abdomen he had a recent splenectomy scar and a palpable tender liver 3 cm below his right costal margin.

1. Suggest three ways in which his present jaundice might be related to his previous accident?
2. What would be the four most useful investigations?

There is a strong possibility that this man's jaundice is related to his previous accident. He must have had transfusions of blood or plasma at the time and a VIRAL HEPATITIS must be a very likely cause of his jaundice. This is likely to be hepatitis B or Non-A, Non-B hepatitis. In addition, there is a type of mononucleosis generally occurring 3–5 weeks after transfusion which is thought, on serological studies, to be due to cytomegalovirus infection. This is often associated with hepatosplenomegaly and hepatic cell damage.

Anyone who has had recent abdominal surgery may develop intra-abdominal sepsis and a SUBPHRENIC ABSCESS or a PYOGENIC LIVER ABSCESS may occur. One must consider the DRUGS he is likely to have received in recent weeks; many tranquillizing drugs (e.g. chlorpromazine or other phenothiazines) can cause jaundice. He has had two anaesthetics and halothane may have been used on both occasions. However, the delay in the onset of his jaundice after his anaesthetic makes this an unlikely cause. Other uncommon causes would be damage to the common bile duct at the time of injury or a Budd-Chiari syndrome due to high platelet levels following splenectomy.

This patient must, therefore, have LIVER FUNCTION TESTS (including a PROTHROMBIN TIME) to define the type of jaundice and degree of liver damage. His HBsAg STATUS must also be determined and blood can also be sent, if necessary, for CMV antibodies. BLOOD CULTURES are necessary, and a subphrenic abscess might be diagnosed by RADIOLOGICAL SCREENING OF THE CHEST. This might show a raised immobile diaphragm on the side of the abscess perhaps with an overlying pleural effusion and/or pulmonary collapse. In addition, gas with a fluid level might be seen below the diaphragm. Alternatively, SIMULTANEOUS LIVER AND LUNG SCANS might show a gap between these two organs due to the abscess, or a cold intrahepatic area may demonstrate an abscess there.

This young man's tranquillizers were stopped. His blood tests showed he was HBsAg positive and he was transferred to an isolation hospital to recover from his type B hepatitis.

Case 65

A 24-year-old newspaper reporter came to Casualty with a three week history of recurrent sore throat, nocturnal sweats, dry cough, occipital headaches and aching muscles. His headaches were on two occasions preceded by episodes of blurred vision. Three days before admission he developed difficulty in passing urine which progressed to urinary retention. At this time he also developed paraesthesiae, weakness in his feet and legs and unsteadiness of gait.

The previous year he had been admitted to hospital with concussion from a car crash. His father had been treated for pulmonary tuberculosis eight years previously.

He was admitted to hospital and catheterised. Over the next two days the paraesthesiae rose to involve the trunk and lower chest and his weakness and unsteadiness progressed so that he could not walk.

On examination, he was pyrexial (37.5°C) with a furred tongue, large tonsils and enlarged lymph glands in his neck. The rest of the abnormal findings were confined to the nervous system: cranial nerves were normal. Despite weakness in both legs, he had normal tone in all four limbs and coordination of the arms was normal. His leg tendon reflexes were increased with extensor plantar reflexes; abdominal reflexes were diminished and cremasteric reflexes were absent. All modalities of sensation were impaired up to T5.

1. Give four possible diagnoses.
2. Give five important investigations.

This young man has a transverse myelitis. However, he has had symptoms above T5 (his two episodes of blurred vision) which suggests a more generalised disease, quite possibly infection in view of the prodromal illness. It is essential with his family history to rule out TUBERCULOUS MENINGITIS and a TUBERCULOUS ABSCESS compressing the spinal cord at T5. A malignant SPACEOCCUPYING LESION must be considered even in the absence of root pain and spinal tenderness. The clinical picture is extremely acute for DISSEMINATED SCLEROSIS, which in its acute form may be associated with optic neuritis (Devic's syndrome). Syphilis may cause a similar picture, but there is no history of contact and no evidence of the rash associated with secondary syphilis. EXANTHEMATA can cause a transverse myelitis, and in this context with lymphadenopathy and large exudative tonsils, infectious mononucleosis is a strong possibility and carries a good prognosis. Measles and mumps are also rare causes and a transverse myelitis is sometimes seen following vaccination.

EXAMINATION OF THE CSF is mandatory in this case for acid fast bacilli, culture, examination of cells, protein and glucose. A CHEST X-RAY may show pulmonary tuberculosis and an X-RAY OF THE DORSAL SPINE may reveal a tuberculous abscess or bone destruction by a space-occupying lesion. Syphilis serology should be carried out in all patients suffering from neurological disease and in this case, a PAUL-BUNNELL and TITRE FOR B VIRUS should be performed. If cord compression is suspected, a MYELOGRAM should be performed and the contrast medium introduced when the lumbar puncture is performed.

Case 66

A 25-year-old airline steward was sent to his GP with low back pain, worse in the mornings, and pain in his left knee. This had started three weeks previously and more recently the backache had radiated to his right leg, and he had developed sore eyes. On direct questioning, he admitted to an episode of diarrhoea about four weeks before. Both his grandfather and uncle had suffered from back trouble.

On examination he had limitation of movement of the lower back due to pain and his left knee was swollen and tender. There was bilateral iritis. Physical examination was otherwise normal.

X-ray of this man's sacro-iliac joints showed sclerosis and erosion of the lower joint margins. X-ray of his lumbar spine was normal.

1. What is the most likely diagnosis?
2. Name four other possible diagnoses.
3. Name three non-musculoskeletal complications of your initial diagnosis.

This man has the feature of ANKYLOSING SPONDYLITIS. As well as the typical backache and sacro-iliitis, this disease may have a peripheral arthritis (usually of the larger joints), iritis, plantar fasciitis and Achilles tendinitis. It has a familial tendency.

Other causes of a seronegative arthritis must, however, be considered – they can all cause back pain and iritis. His episode of diarrhoea raises the possibility of REITER'S DISEASE which may occur after Shigella, Salmonella and Yersinia infections, as well as following non-specific urethritis. In this condition, however, sacro-iliitis is a feature of severe disease and generally occurs late. Gastrointestinal infections can also cause a reactive arthritis without the other features of Reiter's disease. This man's diarrhoea could also be a sign of early ULCERATIVE COLITIS or CROHN'S DISEASE, both of which may be accompanied by a flitting monoarthritis of large joints or by a picture identical to ankylosing spondylitis. The arthropathy may precede the development of other symptoms, as it can also with PSORIATIC ARTHROPATHY. This can take several forms, often being an asymmetrical polyarthritis, an arthritis of distal interphalangeal joints, a picture identical to rheumatoid arthritis or, less commonly, a mutilating arthritis. On occasion, however, it can mimic ankylosing spondylitis. A rare cause of sacro-iliitis is Whipple's disease. Behçet's disease is excluded by the absence of buccal or genital ulceration and other features of the disease, and rheumatoid disease does not cause iritis (it causes a scleritis) and the joint distribution would be most unusual.

Most causes of sacro-iliitis are associated with an increased incidence of the major histocompatibility antigen HLA-B27. This occurs in 8% of Caucasian controls and its incidence varies from 90% in ankylosing spondylitis to 40% in the central form of psoriatic arthritis. There is no correlation with rheumatoid disease or Behçet's syndrome.

Complications of ankylosing spondylitis include AORTIC INCOMPETENCE and CARDIAC CONDUCTION DEFECTS. About 1% of sufferers develop a characteristic UPPER ZONE PULMONARY FIBROSIS. Another rare complication is secondary AMYLOID DISEASE.

Case 67

A 48-year-old welder was admitted as an emergency. While watching television one weekend at home he became gradually more dyspnoeic and coughed up some blood-stained frothy sputum. He had several bouts of chest 'tightness' during the following hour, but dismissed these as being due to 'indigestion'. He had previously been healthy apart from his chronic smoker's cough and an attack of gout 4 years ago. He had had no previous similar episodes and the rest of his family were well.

Examination revealed a dyspnoeic slightly obese man with central cyanosis and sweating. Blood pressure was 140/85 mmHg, pulse 120 per minute, regular and of fair volume. Heart sounds were normal with no added sounds. Venous pressure was not raised, all peripheral pulses were palpable and there was no peripheral oedema. His respiratory rate was raised to 28 per minute, expansion and percussion were normal and throughout the chest there were widespread inspiratory crepitations. Examination of the abdomen, central nervous system and fundi was normal.

Investigations: ECG showed sinus tachycardia, but was otherwise normal. Chest X-ray showed normal cardiac contours without enlargement. There was fluffy shadowing throughout both lung fields, more marked at the periphery and the bases. Kerley B lines were absent and there was no evidence of upper lobe venous diversion. Full blood count, urea and electrolytes were normal.

1. What is the diagnosis?

The patient presents with symptoms and signs suggestive of pulmonary oedema. The commoner causes of this, hypertension, valvular heart disease and myocardial ischaemia, do not appear to be instrumental in the aetiology of this man's illness. He has a normal sized heart, absence of a gallop rhythm and his chest X-ray does not show some of the more usual features of pulmonary venous hypertension. His cardiogram shows no evidence of ischaemia or left ventricular strain and in these circumstances, PULMONARY OEDEMA DUE TO INHALATION OF TOXIC GASES must be considered. His job as a welder may well have exposed him to oxides of nitrogen but can also occur in agriculatural storage silos and in mines following detonations. There may be no immediate symptoms following exposure and pneumonitis and pulmonary oedema may take up to 48 hours to appear. Symptoms depend on the nature of the irritant ranging from fever, headache and a dry cough ('Monday fever' due to zinc oxide poisoning) to asthma (toluene di-isocyanate). In some circumstances, e.g. beryllium inhalation, chronic fibrotic lung disease can occur despite withdrawal from further exposure and nitrous oxide poisoning can be followed by obliterative bronchiolitis and sometimes subsequent bronchiolar fibrosis.

In this case, the diagnosis would be confirmed by the finding of methaemoglobinaemia (due to oxidation of haemoglobin by nitrites and nitrates in the lung) and a recent history of high temperature welding in poorly ventilated surroundings. Management consists of monitoring blood gases, administration of O_2 to correct the inevitable hypoxia and positive pressure ventilation if necessary. Intravenous methylene blue corrects methaemoglobinaemia if present. High dose steroids diminish the inflammatory response which is responsible for the leakage of protein-rich exudate into the alveoli. Diuretics are contraindicated as they may precipitate hypovolaemia.

Case 68

A 50-year-old woman was sent to hospital by her employers, the nuns of a convent where she had lived and worked as a domestic servant since she was a girl of 15.

The patient was mentally subnormal, but was capable of looking after herself and doing simple work. She was cheerful and uncomplaining, but the Mother Superior said she had become more lethargic and easily tired for the previous three months. The patient suffered from grand mal epilepsy for which she took phenobarbitone and phenytoin, but had not taken these regularly and had not bothered to visit her doctor.

On examination she was very pale, mongoloid, had bad teeth, hyperplastic gums, but no lymphadenopathy. She had crepitations at both lung bases and ankle oedema. In her abdomen her liver was not palpable, but the spleen could be tipped.

A blood examination showed: Hb 4.0 g/dl (4 g%), WBC 3.0 × 10⁹/l (3000/mm³), 50% lymphocytes, 38% polymorphs, 6% monocytes and 6% eosinophils. Platelets 40 × 10⁹/l (40 000/mm³), MCV 108 fl /108 μ^3), MCHC 20 mmol/l (33%).

1. What are the two most likely diagnoses?
2. Suggest two other possible diagnoses.
3. Suggest the three most helpful investigations.

The two most likely diagnoses in this patient are FOLATE DEFICIENCY due to poor dietary intake and anticonvulsant therapy, or PERNICIOUS ANAEMIA. Mild degrees of splenomegaly can be associated with any cause of severe megaloblastic anaemia. Another possible, but rare, diagnosis is an aleukaemic presentation of ACUTE MYELOID OR LYMPHATIC LEUKAEMIA, and mongols do have an increased incidence of acute myeloid and lymphatic leukaemia. The anaemia of myxoedema is normally normochromic and normocytic, but 15% of patients have an associated B12 deficiency due to pernicious anaemia. Tuberculosis can cause macrocytosis, but such a severe anaemia in both these causes would not occur without a co-existing deficiency state. Myelofibrosis would not normally fit into this clinical picture, particularly with such a relatively small spleen.

The three most helpful investigations would be A BONE MARROW, RED CELL FOLATE, and SERUM B12. Further investigations might include a Schilling test and thyroid function.

The patient had, in fact, pernicious anaemia.

Case 69

A woman of 55 attended the chest clinic. 30 years before she had had a thoracoplasty for pulmonary tuberculosis. She smoked heavily and always had a productive cough. Apart from several haemoptyses over the years she had been well, but recently her shortness of breath had become worse and she had had a further haemoptysis. Her left wrist was swollen and tender and she was taking aspirin to relieve the pain.

On examination she was cyanosed, dyspnoeic and febrile. There was a right thoracoplasty scar and the trachea deviated to the right. In the right upper zone there was dullness to percussion, an area of bronchial breathing and coarse crepitations. Her fingers were clubbed.

1. Suggest two possible causes for her repeated haemoptyses over the years.
2. What are the four possible causes for her present illness?
3. Give two reasons for her swollen wrist.

By the removal of several ribs a thoracoplasty allowed the chest wall to collapse and obliterate a tuberculous cavity. It was an effective and time-honoured treatment that has now been superseded by modern chemotherapy but, nevertheless, there are still many people who have had their pulmonary tuberculosis treated this way. Residual BRONCHIECTASIS is common in these patients and this, or a reactivation of their quiescent TUBERCULOSIS, may lead to fresh haemoptyses. Rarely fungi colonise damaged parts of the lung and the resulting mycetoma will manifest itself by recurrent haemoptyses.

This woman now has a febrile illness associated with signs of collapse and consolidation in the right lung. An ACUTE INFECTION is the most likely diagnosis but BRONCHIAL CARCINOMA, PULMONARY EMBOLUS or reactivation of the TUBERCULOSIS must be considered.

The wrist swelling might be due to a TUBERCULOUS ARTHRITIS or HYPERTROPHIC PULMONARY OSTEOARTHROPATHY. This is frequently associated with bronchial carcinoma but is sometimes also seen with long-standing bronchiectasis, or other conditions including Crohn's disease, primary biliary cirrhosis and cyanotic congenital heart disease.

Case 70

A 24-year-old student went to see his general practitioner with a three week history of low back pain, especially in the mornings. On questioning, he admitted that he had had difficulty playing games at school through back trouble, but until the present exacerbation this had improved. In addition, he had visited his general practitioner occasionally with abdominal discomfort and diarrhoea for which he had been given Colofac with no real success.

On examination, he was pyrexial and anaemic. The only other abnormal physical sign was that he had a tender palpable mass in the right iliac fossa. Rectal examination and sigmoidoscopy were normal. He had tenderness on flexion of his lumbo-sacral spine.

Initial investigations: Hb 9.0 g/dl (9.0 g%), ESR 60 mm/h, WBC 10.0×10^9/l (10 000/mm^3), stool culture and microscopy negative.

1. Give your diagnosis and two other possibilities.
2. Suggest five further investigations.

The most likely situation in this young man is inflammatory disease of the bowel associated with inflammatory joint disease affecting his lumbo-sacral spine. This association points towards CROHN'S DISEASE which may present as a mass in the right iliac fossa. ILEOCAECAL TUBERCULOSIS may also present in this fashion if there is associated tubercular disease of the spine. The only malignant type of disease which is likely to present in this way and in this age group would be a LYMPHOMA OF THE SMALL BOWEL metastasising to the lumbo-sacral spine. Ulcerative colitis may also present with inflammatory bowel disease and spondylitis. It is extremely rare, however, for it to present as a mass in the right iliac fossa and it is also very unusual to have a normal sigmoidoscopy. An appendix abscess could present in this way and also actinomycosis, but neither could explain the back symptoms.

Investigations must include a CHEST X-RAY, X-RAY OF THE LUMBOSACRAL SPINE AND SACROILIAC JOINTS to look for spondylitis or possible tuberculous or lymphomatous involvement of these areas. BARIUM STUDIES should be performed to look for disease in the bowel, in particular the ileo-caecal area. A RECTAL BIOPSY might show typical features of Crohn's Disease and if tuberculosis is really suggested, then acid fast bacilli should be sought with cultures of stool, early morning urine and gastric washings. If these do not give a firm diagnosis, LAPAROTOMY may be necessary. An isotopic bone scan might be helpful in the further investigation of his back symptoms.

Case 71

A 34-year-old woman was pregnant for the first time. For four years she had been treated for mild hypertension by her family practitioner and at the time of her first visit to the antenatal clinic, her blood pressure was 150/100 mmHg and she was taking hydrochlorothiazide (25 mg daily). The drug was changed to alpha-methyldopa on which her blood pressure was well controlled until 32 weeks gestation when the pressure rose to 180/110 mmHg and she developed peripheral oedema.

She was admitted to hospital and hydralazine (25 mg twice daily) was added to the treatment which temporarily controlled the pressure but she went into premature labour.

An intravenous salbutamol infusion was set up in an attempt to suppress uterine contractions. Shortly thereafter, she developed acute pulmonary oedema.

1. How do you account for the development of pulmonary oedema?
2. What important physical sign should have been recorded?
3. What therapeutic error was made?

It is probable that the precipitation of left ventricular failure in this woman was a result of the intravenous infusion of salbutamol and might have been avoided if the PULSE RATE had been recorded prior to the infusion. Reference to the patient's charts showed that the heart rate was 120 per minute at this time and rose rapidly with the salbutamol.

A number of factors were undoubtedly contributory to the onset of pulmonary oedema. The blood pressure reduction that occurs with the vasodilator drug hydralazine is accompanied by a reflexly mediated rise in heart rate, in addition to salt and water retention. Infusing a drug which, despite its claimed selectivity for beta$_2$ receptors, undoubtedly had an effect on the heart, would have an additive effect and lead to a progressive rise in heart rate.

Contributory factors resulting in the development of heart failure include the high output state characteristic of late pregnancy, the increased circulatory blood volume and the obvious fluid retention.

In this case, the high pulse rate should have alerted the obstetrician to the potential hazard that could be encountered with a beta-stimulant drug and SALBUTAMOL SHOULD NOT HAVE BEEN GIVEN.

Alpha-methyldopa has been implicated in this drug interaction, although the mechanism remains obscure.

Case 72

A woman of 68 (a well-known public figure) was referred for a medical opinion by the ophthalmic department who had noticed her to have abnormal pupils at a routine examination. The patient said her only complaint was some tingling and numbness in the right index and middle fingers for two or three years and she sometimes had difficulty in picking up small objects with that hand. A doctor had told her that her pupils were abnormal at least ten years previously. Almost 30 years ago she had had a partial thyroidectomy for a toxic goitre but had never had anything else wrong with her.

Abnormal findings were limited to the nervous system. Her pupils were small and showed no reaction to light, but reacted to accommodation. The other cranial nerves were normal. Her ankle jerks and left knee jerk were absent but all sensory modalities were normal in her legs. There was some generalised loss of sensation in the right thumb, index and middle fingers with slight wasting of the adductor pollicus brevis. Otherwise there were no abnormal findings.

1. Give the two most likely explanations for her pupil abnormalities.
2. What is the probable cause of the symptoms in her right hand, and give two useful investigations in your management.

This woman's pupillary reactions could be due to either ARGYLL ROBERTSON pupils or bilateral ADIE'S TONIC pupils. The former are found in tertiary syphilis and rarely in diabetes mellitus. Adie's pupils can be bilateral in a substantial number of patients and, although initially they are dilated, with time they become miosed. There is usually some preservation of the light reflex but this can be difficult to see and careful examination of the near reflex is necessary to pick up the tonic response. The lesion lies in the ciliary ganglion. Adie's pupils are frequently associated with loss of knee and ankle jerks and sometimes upper limb reflexes, but there is never any sensory disturbance. The diagnosis can be confirmed by demonstrating hypersensitivity to weak pilocarpine drops. The diagnosis of Adie's pupils in this patient spared her a lumbar puncture which would otherwise have been a necessity.

Her hand symptoms were due to a CARPAL TUNNEL SYNDROME. This was confirmed by showing delayed conduction on ELECTROMYOGRAPHY. A carpal tunnel syndrome can be associated with myxoedema and in view of her previous partial thyroidectomy, THYROID FUNCTION TESTS were done which were, however, normal. A Horner's syndrome can follow thyroid surgery, but of course these pupils retain normal light and near reflexes.

Case 73

A 22-year-old Irish girl was well until twelve months before, when she started to become short of breath on effort and latterly this had been associated with tightness across the upper chest. There was no history of rheumatic heart disease and she had never been cyanosed. Five years previously she had applied to work as a cook in a London hospital and no abnormality had been found at the medical examination. She did not smoke and drank only rarely. Her mother was alive and well, but her father had collapsed and died suddenly when she was a young girl. She had two younger brothers who were both well.

On examination, she was not anaemic or clubbed. The pulse was 80 per minute, regular and jerky, but sustained in nature. The blood pressure was 120/70 mm Hg, and her venous pressure was not raised. The cardiac apex was not displaced and was double in character. Cardiac auscultation revealed normal first and second heart sounds and both a fourth heart sound and late systolic murmur were audible at the apex. The lung fields were clear.

Investigations: Chest X-ray showed a normal heart size. ECG showed Q waves in leads V2–V6 with changes of left ventricular hypertrophy. Full blood count, serum lipids, thyroid function and syphilis serology were normal.

1. What is the diagnosis?
2. How would you confirm this and what abnormalities would you expect to find?
3. What is the cause of her double apical impulse?
4. How would you treat the girl?

This girl presents with symptoms of angina pectoris at an unusually early age and no risk factors apart, perhaps, from her father's early death. This makes her angina unlikely to be due to coronary artery disease and the abnormalities on examination support this. She has signs typical of HYPERTROPHIC OBSTRUCTIVE CARDIOMYOPATHY (HOCM), a disorder which must always be considered in the differential diagnosis of angina.

Her jerky pulse is due to a rapid initial upstroke followed by the development of left ventricular outflow obstruction causing a small sustained second component. The double apical impulse is a palpable atrial filling thrust – increased to overcome the resistance to left ventricular filling caused by the cardiomyopathy. The late systolic murmur is due to outflow tract obstruction distorting the mitral valve and causing regurgitation.

Diagnostic confirmation is usually via ECHOCARDIOGRAPHY which may reveal:
a. A greatly thickened septum (>1.3 cm) with a ratio of septal to posterior wall thickness of >1.5 cm.
b. Systolic anterior motion of the anterior mitral valve leaflet.
c. Mid-systolic closure of the aortic valve.
It will rarely be necessary to proceed to left ventricular angiography which shows a bent slit-like, 'tear-drop' left ventricular cavity.

The mainstay of treatment is with BETA-ADRENERGIC BLOCKING DRUGS which allow improved ventricular filling and decrease the outflow tract obstruction. Many patients improve symptomatically on therapy, but there is no definite evidence that it prevents ventricular arrhythmias and sudden death to which they are prone. HOCM is usually inherited as an autosomal dominant condition and this girl's father no doubt died suddenly because he was also a sufferer. The rest of the family should also be screened with echocardiography.

If patients do not respond to beta-adrenergic blockers and have persistent outflow tract gradients, then surgery can be performed to resect the septal hypertrophy. Mitral valve replacement may also be necessary. The operation has a significant mortality and morbidity.

Case 74

The patient, a 45-year-old salesman, had been admitted to hospital with an attack of left sided pleuritic pain, which had lasted for 24 hours and then subsided. At that time, he had been well apart from severe but fleeting pains in his wrists which he had attributed to 'rheumatism'. He smoked 10 cigarettes a day.

Examination at that time showed no abnormalities apart from the signs of a small left sided pleural effusion and mild synovial swelling in both wrists. There was no evidence of venous thrombosis in the legs.

Investigation at that time showed a normal blood count, electrolytes and sputum culture. Sputum cytology was negative for malignant cells. Aspiration of the pleural effusion demonstrated clear yellow fluid, protein content 35 g/l, which contained no cells and was sterile on culture (including Löwenstein-Jensen culture). X-ray of the wrists was normal and chest X-ray showed the small effusion, but was otherwise normal. He was followed up in the Chest Clinic and the radiological appearances remained unchanged.

Four months later, he was admitted as an emergency in a confused state. He had become increasingly agitated over three days and was expressing paranoid ideas about his wife's infidelity with the local greengrocer. This patient was afebrile with no papilloedema or neurological signs.

Subsequent investigation showed: Hb 13.4 g/dl (13.4 g%), WBC 3.0×10^9/l (3000/mm³), platelets 320×10^9/l (320 000/mm³), ESR 80 mm/h. Urea and electrolytes were normal. Blood sugar 6.4 mmol/l (115 mg%). Calcium 2.38 mmol/l (9.52 mg%), WR was negative. Radioisotope brain scan was normal. Lumbar puncture was performed and showed an opening pressure of 14 cm H_2O. Examination showed 40 lymphocytes per cubic millimetre, no malignant cells, gram stain negative, protein 0.8 g/l (80 mg%), sugar 5 mmol/l (90 mg%). The chest X-ray appearances of the pleural effusion were unchanged. No parenchymal lung lesion was seen.

1. What is the diagnosis?
2. Give one investigation to confirm it.

The cause of this patient's pleural effusion remained unknown despite investigation. Pneumonia and pulmonary infarction are unlikely, but malignancy and tuberculosis are both very real possibilities, especially in view of the subsequent confusional state. Tuberculous effusions may be difficult to diagnose and positive culture may only be obtained in 25% of cases. However, the subsequent mental picture and CSF findings are unlikely to be explained by tuberculous meningitis, although cultures for tuberculosis should certainly be set up. A malignant effusion is unlikely in view of the static nature of the chest X-ray and negative sputum cytology.

There are a number of causes of mental changes in patients with carcinoma of the bronchus, including frontal lobe secondaries, hyponatraemia (usually due to inappropriate ADH secretion), hypercalcaemia (bone secondaries or ectopic parathyroid hormone production), or a non-metastatic encephalopathy. Painful wrists in a patient with a possible pulmonary neoplasm suggests hypertrophic pulmonary osteoarthropathy, but X-ray of the wrists did not show subperiosteal new bone formation. However, arthritis and pleural involvement raise the possibility of a connective tissue disorder, which taken in conjunction with a confusional state and a mild leucopenia, is strongly suggestive of SYSTEMIC LUPUS ERYTHEMATOSUS. This should be confirmed by the finding of raised titre of ANTI-DNA ANTIBODIES.

Cerebral involvement in systemic lupus erythematosus is common, usually manifesting as epilepsy or psychiatric changes. This latter occurs in up to 60% of patients and may vary from mild behavioural disturbances to a florid psychosis. The pathological change is thought to be a vasculitis of the cerebral arteries and normally responds well to steroids. Other neurological manifestations include peripheral neuropathy, myelopathy, hemiplegia and chorea.

Case 75

A 72-year-old retired school teacher had been on 10 mg prednisone daily for two years to control her temporal arteritis when she was seen complaining of sudden severe backache which had started two days previously. The pain was severe, radiating to her left groin and worse on coughing or movement.

Apart from her temporal arteritis she had always been well and took no drugs other than her steroids. She did not smoke or drink.

When examined she seemed well and cheerful. There was some pallor of her mucous membranes and tenderness over her spine in the area of T10 to 11. The spleen could just be tipped but otherwise examination was normal.

Investigations showed: chest X-ray normal; spinal X-rays showed collapse of the vertebral bodies of T10 and T11; Hb 9.9 g/dl (9.9 g%), WBC 9.0 × 10⁹/l (9000/mm³), ESR 8 mm/h, PCV 0.31 (31%), MCV 120 fl (120 μ³), MCHC 20 mmol/l (32%), reticulocytes 7%, platelets 273 × 10⁹/l (273 000/mm³), serum iron 18.8 μ mol/l (105 μ g%), TIBC 45.0 μ mol/l (251 μ g%), bilirubin 20 μ mol/l (1.2 mg%), aspartate transaminase 40 U/l, alkaline phosphatase 98 U/l, urea 8.3 mmol/l (50 mg%), plasma sodium 140 mmol/l (140 mEq/l), potassium 3.7 mmol/l (3.7 mEq/l), WR positive, treponema immobilisation test negative, ANF negative, proteins 72 g/l (7.2%), albumin 39 g/l (3.9 g%), MSU sterile, urobilinogen positive, haemoglobin negative.

1. What are the two most likely reasons for her vertebral collapse?
2. What are the four most useful investigations to define the cause of her anaemia?

This woman might have collapsed her vertebrae through STEROID ENHANCED OSTEOPOROSIS or NEOPLASTIC DEPOSITS.

The blood tests indicate that she has a haemolytic anaemia associated with a false positive WR. Apart from showing hyperplasia, a bone marrow, although unlikely to aid in the diagnosis of the cause of the anaemia, should be performed and her PERIPHERAL BLOOD examined for signs of a microangiopathic picture with its grossly deformed red cells.

At this age her haemolytic anaemia must surely be acquired and in the absence of any significant drug history or chronic infection one must look for associated antibodies. She could have a DIRECT COOMB'S TEST for warm antibodies. COLD AGGLUTININS and an ELECTROPHORESIS for abnormal proteins, which are usually of the IgM class, should be sought. HAM'S TEST FOR ACID HAEMOLYSIS will identify the rare cases of paroxysmal nocturnal haemoglobinuria which is due to an acquired red cell defect.

The direct Coomb's test was positive in this patient. About 50% of patients with a haemolytic anaemia associated with warm antibodies have underlying disorders, either collagen diseases, lymphomas or malignancy.

The bone scan suggested more neoplastic deposits in the spine and the lesion at T10 was needle biopsied under X-ray control. This confirmed the diagnosis of neoplasia. A few months later the patient died from her ovarian carcinoma.

Case 76

A 32-year-old woman teacher presented with a three month history of episodes of transient painless vertical diplopia. The double vision was worse on looking up and to the right, the attacks lasted for several hours and tended to happen more towards the end of the day. Apart from feeling more tired recently (which she ascribed to the imminence of the A level exams) she was otherwise well. Three years previously she had had a partial thyroidectomy for primary hyperthyroidism and since then had been taking 0.1 mg thyroxine daily.

On examination she had normal visual acuities. Her pupils were equal and the reflexes normal. There was partial ptosis of the right upper lid, the left was normal. Ocular movements of the right eye were limited in elevation, the left were full. Optic discs and visual fields were full. General examination was otherwise normal.

Investigations: Hb 11.2 g/dl (11.2 g%), WBC 6.5 × 10⁹/l (6500/mm³), ESR 15 mm/h. Urea 4.2 mmol/l (25 mg%), plasma sodium 137 mmol/l (137 mEq/l, plasma potassium 3.7 mmol/l (3.7 mEq/l), serum calcium 2.4 mmol/l (9.6 mg%), serum T4 slightly low, T3 normal. Skull and chest X-rays were normal.

1. What is the most likely diagnosis?
2. How would you confirm this?
3. If this was normal what other diagnosis would you consider?

This lady presents with transient vertical diplopia which is due to the inability to elevate her right eye, and a ptosis. In spite of her previous hyperthyroidism, thyroid eye disease is a most unlikely cause of her diplopia as it virtually never produces a ptosis.

In any transient or variable ptosis, MYASTHENIA GRAVIS must be considered, there is an association with thyroid disease and it is the most likely diagnosis in this patient. She should have a TENSILON TEST which must be performed with caution as respiratory or cardiovascular collapse is unfortunately not uncommon following this test and nasty accidents do happen. Some authorities recommend observing the effect of a control injection of saline followed by a test dose of 1–2 mg of Tensilon. If available, acetyl choline receptor antibodies should be looked for as they are a reliable indicator of myasthenia gravis, although they can sometimes be negative when the myasthenia is limited to the ocular muscles. An EMG should show fatiguability; single fibre studies are helpful, but these require a stoical patient and are time consuming. Mediastinal tomography and CT scanning will indicate whether a thymoma is present; the presence of striated muscle antibodies is said to correlate with this.

Other causes of her diplopia include a PARTIAL 3rd NERVE PALSY; the absence of pain and pupillary involvement are against compression of the nerve from a posterior communicating artery aneurysm. The lesion in this patient would be isolated to the superior division of the third nerve and would probably be located in the superior ophthalmic fissure. Local orbital infiltrations or a sphenoidal ridge meningioma would be possible causes, although one might expect the patient to have some pain and proptosis from these. Skull X-ray and an orbital CT scan would show the lesion; sometimes inflammation from an infected frontal sinus can produce this picture. Familial ocular myopathies are usually symmetrical and the normality of the other eye excludes these conditions. The Eaton-Lambert syndrome never affects ocular muscles.

Case 77

A 30-year-old woman was referred for a physician's opinion by the local optician. She had gone there for a new pair of glasses as she thought that eyestrain was responsible for her recent headaches. At that time she was found to have marked optic disc swelling in her left eye and a suspicion of this in the right. Past medical history was unremarkable, but for the past two years she had been seeing a psychiatrist for depression and marital problems. Her periods were somewhat irregular and she had recently put on weight. She was on no medication and neither drank nor smoked.

On examination, her blood pressure was 140/90 mmHg. There were no abnormal physical findings apart from her obesity and optic disc swelling. Her visual acuity and fields were normal (apart from enlarged blind spots). She was depressed and was convinced that she was going to die.

1. How would you confirm that the right optic disc was swollen?
2. What is the most likely diagnosis?
3. Suggest the three most useful investigations in reaching the diagnosis.

Optic discs can be swollen from many causes and these days papilloedema implies swelling from raised CSF pressure. Confirmation that this patient has bilateral papilloedema is readily and simply shown by FLUORESCEIN ANGIOGRAPHY of the fundus – the suspected optic disc will leak dye if it is swollen. Many patients might be spared unnecessary and dangerous investigations by this simple test.

In a young person who has an unremarkable history together with essentially normal physical findings apart from obesity and papilloedema, some evidence of endocrine imbalance and a normal blood pressure, BENIGN INTRACRANIAL HYPERTENSION must be the most likely diagnosis. However, this is a diagnosis of exclusion requiring full investigation to exclude a space-occupying lesion or obstructive hydrocephalus. The essential investigations are a SKULL X-RAY and a COMPUTERISED AXIAL TOMOGRAPHIC SCAN. If the CT scan is normal with small or normal sized ventricles, a LUMBAR PUNCTURE should be performed to measure pressure and confirm that the cytology and biochemistry of the CSF is normal. Bilateral carotid angiography is only indicated if a mass lesion is shown on scanning and air encephalography has been superseded by CT scanning. A SERUM CALCIUM and SEROLOGY FOR SYPHILIS would be useful.

The CSF pressure can usually be controlled by carbonic anhydrase inhibitors, e.g. acetazolamide, but repeated lumbar punctures are sometimes used. The most serious complication of benign intracranial hypertension is progressive visual failure due to chronic unrelieved papilloedema and decompression of the optic nerves or lumbar-peritoneal shunting is then required.

Benign intracranial hypertension can be associated with a variety of conditions namely obesity, the oral contraceptive pill, steroid treatment or withdrawal, middle ear disease, head trauma, hypervitaminosis A and hypocalcaemia. The condition has also been recorded following the use of nalidixic acid, nitrofurantoin and tetracyclines.

Case 78

A 64-year-old woman had the following past history. She had developed
rheumatic fever after her first pregnancy when she was 25. She was rested in bed
for 3 months, treated with aspirin, and made a good recovery. Six years later,
during her second pregnancy, she became dyspnoeic on exertion, developed
cardiac failure and recurrent small haemoptyses. 4 years later, when she was 35,
she had sudden onset of pain in both legs which became white, cold and pale.
The condition improved over the next 36 hours. The following year she had three
attacks of pneumonia and a bowel resection for a mesenteric embolus. Histology
showed a normal thrombus. When the patient was 41, she had a mitral valvotomy
to relieve her orthopnoea and dyspnoea on minimal exertion and after this she was
able to walk two miles. She remained well but developed the murmurs of mitral
and tricuspid incompetence as well as her mitral stenosis. When she was 60 she
had an episode of severe central chest pain in bed lasting 5 hours. She was
anticoagulated but two months later she had an episode of left loin pain and frank
haematuria. Anticoagulants were stopped.

1. What was the most likely cause of haemoptysis in the second pregnancy?
2. What was the cause of her leg symptoms when she was 35?
3. What are the three most likely causes of her chest pain when she was 60?
4. What are the two most likely causes of the haematuria?
5. What are the likely ECG abnormalities this patient would show before her
   episode of chest pain four years ago?

There are four reasons why haemoptyses may occur more commonly in patients with mitral stenosis:

1. VENOUS ENGORGEMENT OCCURS IN THE PULMONARY VASCULAR BED as a consequence of the high left atrial pressure. These veins may rupture causing haemoptysis. Pathologically haemosiderin is deposited in the lungs causing mottling on the chest X-ray and which may eventually calcify.
2. PULMONARY OEDEMA may occur with the expectoration of blood stained frothy sputum.
3. PULMONARY EMBOLI are more frequent, presumably due to decreased cardiac output and less active lifestyles of the patients.
4. There is an increased incidence of CHEST INFECTIONS.

In addition, the patient may have an increased bleeding tendency through the use of ANTICOAGULANTS. In this patient the most likely cause of her early haemoptyses would be her pulmonary venous engorgement.

Embolisation may occur at any stage of her disease, but especially after the onset of atrial fibrillation, which often marks an increase in the patient's deterioration. This woman has a SADDLE EMBOLUS BLOCKING THE BIFURCATION OF THE AORTA. If a patient presents with embolisation requiring surgical removal, then the embolus must be sent for histology to exclude a left atrial myxoma which may give identical cardiac signs. Embolisation must also raise the possibility of infective endocarditis, although this is a rare complication of pure mitral stenosis.

Her chest pain at the age of 60 might have been due to PULMONARY EMBOLISM or a MYOCARDIAL INFARCTION. The latter may be due to a CORONARY EMBOLUS as well as secondary to atheroma.

Her haematuria may well have resulted from OVER-ANTICOAGULATION or from a RENAL EMBOLUS.

In the ECG, the earliest sign is that of P mitrale if the patient is in sinus rhythm. This, of course, disappears with the onset of atrial fibrillation. As the mitral stenosis advances, there may be changes of RIGHT VENTRICULAR HYPERTROPHY and RIGHT AXIS DEVIATION.

Case 79

A 20-year-old girl was admitted to hospital in a state of collapse with a history of malaise and lethargy for two days associated with vomiting. On the day of admission she complained of a severe headache and weakness. She had become confused and disoriented and vomited profusely.

Examination showed delirium, dehydration, a tachycardia of 140 per minute, blood pressure of 110/60 mmHg, temperature 36°C. Purpuric areas were identified on the arms. There was neck stiffness, a positive Kernig's sign and signs of cerebral irritability. The optic discs were pink with early papilloedema. Reflexes were normal and the plantar response showed a marked withdrawal reaction. The right knee joint was swollen, hot and tender.

Investigations: Hb 13 g/dl (13 g%), WBC 25×10^9/l (25 000/mm^3), neutrophils 19.7×10^9/l (19 700/mm^3), platelets 20×10^9/l (20 000/mm^3), plasma sodium 137 mmol/l (137 mEq/l), potassium 3.4 mmol/l (3.4 mEq/l), bicarbonate 16 mmol/l (16 mEq/l), urea 18.2 mmol/l (110 mg%). CSF: pressure raised. WBC 3.5×10^9/l (3500/mm^3), polymorphs 100%. RBC 1.2×10^9/l (1250/mm^3). No organisms seen. Protein 0.8 g/l (800 mg%). Sugar less than 0.25 mmol/l (5 mg%).

1. What would be your initial therapy?
2. What agent do you suspect is responsible for her meningitis?
3. What complication do you suspect might be present?
4. What would be the two most useful tests to confirm this?
5. Give two possible causes for her swollen right knee.

This girl is seriously ill with meningitis and the clinical picture and CSF findings indicate a bacterial infection. Although the organisms were not identified on initial gram stains of the spinal fluid, the most likely causative agent in this case is the MENINGOCOCCUS. However, infection with pneumococcus or haemophilus influenzae must be considered.

General treatment consists of the correction of fluid and electrolyte deficits, adequate oxygenation and maintenance of cardiovascular function. Specific antibiotic regimes vary but drugs should be started immediately in high doses and intravenously. They should cover all likely organisms and suggested regimes are PENICILLIN and CHLORAMPHENICOL (with or without a sulphonamide) or AMPICILLIN. Many strains of the meningococcus are now resistant to sulphonamides and ampicillin resistant haemophilus strains are now present, especially in the U.S.A.

Although the meningococcaemia may be associated with many skin manifestations including rose spots, petechiae and frank purpura, the co-existence of severe thrombocytopenia and bruising suggests the possibility of DISSEMINATED INTRAVASCULAR COAGULATION, which should be investigated by CLOTTING STUDIES and examination of the serum for FIBRINOGEN DEGRADATION PRODUCTS. It may be necessary to correct the clotting abnormalities by the use of blood products and some would give heparin in an attempt to stop the coagulation although there is no evidence that it improves the outcome in such cases.

Acute cerebral oedema may be life-threatening and require treatment with mannitol or dexamethasone. Many would also give steroid therapy to the seriously ill patient with no evidence of cerebral oedema, especially in view of the possibility of haemorrhage into the adrenal glands. Again there is no definite evidence of benefit.

The swollen right knee could reflect a PYOGENIC ARTHRITIS, consequent upon septicaemia, but the possibility of a HAEMARTHROSIS should be entertained, although this is an unusual manifestation of disseminated intravascular coagulation. A sterile polyarthropathy may be found in meningococcal infections, although this usually occurs in conjunction with a chronic meningococcaemia.

Case 80

A 65-year-old Scottish woman was admitted as a surgical emergency with a four day history of vomiting, diarrhoea and upper abdominal pain. She had previously been well except for recent weight loss and lethargy.

On examination she was dark skinned, but pale, and had patches of vitiligo. She was dehydrated, shocked, her pulse rapid and weak and she had generalised abdominal tenderness.

Initial investigations showed a Hb of 14.5 g/dl (14.5 g%); WBC 18 × 10⁹/l (18 000/mm³); plasma sodium 137 mmol/l (137 mEq/l); potassium 8.8 mmol/l (8.8 mEq/l); chloride 100 mmol/l (100 mEq/l); bicarbonate 8 mmol/l (8 mEq/l); blood sugar 33.3 mmol/l (600 mg%); urea 32.2 mmol/l (194 mg%); amylase normal. Abdominal X-ray (erect and supine) showed no evidence of gas under the diaphragm. The ECG revealed peaked T waves, but no evidence of infarction.

Initial treatment was rehydration, insulin, antibiotics and hydrocortisone and she improved gradually. Three days later while continuing to improve she was on a carbohydrate restricted diet, oral fluids and insulin, she remained hypotensive.

Investigations at this time revealed plasma sodium 124 mmol/l (124 mEq/l); potassium 4.1 mmol/l (4.1 mEq/l); chloride 101 mmol/l (101 mEq/l); bicarbonate 19.7 mmol/l (19.7 mEq/l); blood sugar 8.6 mmol/l (156 mg%); urea 23.5 mmol/l (140 mg%).

1. From what four conditions does this patient suffer?
2. What would be the three most useful investigations on recovery?

At the time of admission this woman was referred to the surgical team with a provisional diagnosis of a perforated peptic ulcer or acute pancreatitis, neither of which were born out by subsequent investigations. She had undoubted DIABETIC KETOACIDOSIS with gross dehydration and renal failure. Diabetic ketoacidosis is frequently precipitated by an underlying infection or a myocardial infarction, and here an infection was thought to be the likely cause, though no primary focus was apparent. She was thought to be septicaemic with shock and she was treated with broad spectrum antibiotics and steroids.

The combination of pigmentation, vitiligo and hypotension, associated with a previous history of abdominal pain is strongly suggestive of Addison's disease. The subsequent finding of hyponatraemia supports this concept. Therefore, the most likely explanation of the initial presentation is that she had diabetic ketoacidosis, ADDISONIAN CRISIS, RENAL FAILURE with possibly a marked pre-renal element and SEPTICAEMIA, and the fortuitous administration of hydrocortisone initially masked the Addisonian component.

Further investigations should include assessment of adrenal function. The patient should be treated with DEXAMETHASONE and a SYNACTHEN STIMULATION TEST should be performed to assess adrenal responsiveness and ADRENAL ANTIBODIES should be sought. Once fully replaced with steroids, the renal function should be assessed by doing a CREATININE CLEARANCE to see the degree, if any, of primary renal disease.

The association of Addison's disease and diabetes mellitus is well recognised.

Case 81

A 26-year-old school teacher was first seen by her general practitioner for vaccination prior to a holiday in Egypt. She was normally well and he was therefore surprised to see her again shortly after her return. She stated that during her holiday she had developed severe pain in her right shoulder and upper arm which lasted 3–4 days but subsided shortly before her return. Following this she had noticed difficulty in brushing her hair and raising her arm above her head.

The general practitioner referred her to the local hospital where she was found to have weakness and wasting of the deltoid and serratus anterior muscles on that side, together with some sensory loss over the lateral aspect of the shoulder.

1. What is the diagnosis?
2. What is the treatment and prognosis?

This lady describes the typical history of NEURALGIC AMYOTROPHY (ACUTE BRACHIAL NEURITIS) which may occur spontaneously or following trauma, infections, or, as in her case, vaccinations.

In the acute painful stage, the differential diagnosis must include an ACUTE RADICULAR SYNDROME due to cervical disc degeneration but at her age this would be unlikely and her subsequent weakness does not follow a root distribution. An ACUTE INFLAMMATORY MYOPATHY may start locally with muscle pain and swelling but would generally progress to a more symmetrical and typical clinical picture. Such disease is often idiopathic but may occur in association with a viral infection, malignancy or a collagen vascular disease. A myopathy would not explain her area of sensory loss.

TRAUMA to the upper trunk of the brachial plexus is not uncommon in people carrying heavy loads in a rucksack. It causes proximal muscle weakness and sensory loss on the outer side of the arm, but would not cause the more localised weakness of this lady nor her preceding pain.

HERPES ZOSTER would cause pain and occasionally causes localised muscle weakness and wasting due to anterior horn cell involvement. Here, however, there is no rash and the selective muscle involvement would be unusual.

Although the weakness and wasting in patients with an acute brachial neuritis may persist for long periods, the condition is benign and in most cases recovery is eventually complete. Corticosteroid therapy may be used which probably does not influence the course of the illness, but may relieve the pain. Recurrent attacks have been described.

Case 82

A 79-year-old woman was referred from the eye clinic. She had presented complaining of floaters in her vision and was found to have the fundal appearance of retinal vein obstruction.

She said she had been short of breath for a month after walking twenty or thirty yards and felt too weak to do her housework. She lived in a ground floor flat. Her appetite was poor and she had lost about a stone in weight over the previous three months. Direct questioning revealed that she had had frequent recent nose bleeds and that her fingers became white in cold weather.

On examination she was plethoric. She had a regular pulse of 80, blood pressure 140/100 mmHg with an ejection systolic murmur at the apex. She could lie flat with no dyspnoea. In her abdomen the liver was palpable 2 cm and spleen 3 cm. There was no lymphadenopathy and apart from the fundal appearances examination was otherwise normal.

1. From this history alone what are the three most likely diagnoses?

In Outpatients, blood examination showed Hb 8.7 g/dl (8.7 g%), MCHC 30 g/dl (30%), MCH 30 fl (30 μ^3), platelets 109×10^9/l (109 000/mm³), ESR 260 (calculated), film-rouleaux and plasma cells. Later the MSU urea and electrolytes, calcium, phosphate and hepatic enzymes were found to be normal.

1. Suggest three possible complications of the most likely diagnosis that this patient may have.
3. What would be your urgent management?
4. What would be the three most relevant investigations?

This woman has a mild malaise associated with hepatosplenomegaly. From her history the diagnosis lay between WALDENSTROM'S MACROGLOBULINAEMIA, a LYMPHOMA and POLYCYTHAEMIA RUBRA VERA which would be unusual at this age. Myeloma would be unlikely with the absence of bone pain with liver and spleen involvement.

Patients with macroglobulinaemia may develop a HYPERVISCOSITY syndrome due to their high levels of plasma globulins. This is thought to cause the fundal appearances, malaise and sometimes neurological sequelae resulting from cerebral thromboses. BLEEDING EPISODES are common due to plasma protein, clotting factor and platelet interactions and her RAYNAUD'S PHENOMENON is probably due to cryoglobulins. Occasionally AMYLOIDOSIS may involve the parenchymal organs.

This patient's hyperviscosity threatens her vision and she requires urgent PLASMAPHORESIS to remove the excess protein from her blood.

To establish a diagnosis a BONE MARROW, PLASMA PROTEIN estimation and IMMUNOPHORESIS are necessary. Her globulin level was 90 g/l (9 g%) with the abnormal protein confined to the IgM band.

Case 83

A 50-year-old tramp was admitted to hospital with a four week history of anorexia and persistent cough. On several occasions the sputum had contained blood and in addition, he admitted to recent night sweats and malaise. He smoked 1 oz of tobacco a day and drank as much cheap sherry as he could afford.

Chest X-ray showed collapse of the right upper lobe and a cavity in the anterior segment of the upper lobe. The left upper lobe showed fibrosis and calcification. Ziehl-Neelsen staining of sputum showed acid-fast bacilli. He was started on rifampicin, ethambutol and isoniazid, but he continued to feel unwell and lose weight. Two months later, his chest X-ray showed further collapse of the right upper lobe and persistence of the cavity. Six sputum cultures on Löwenstein-Jensen media were sterile after six weeks' incubation.

1. What is the most likely diagnosis?
2. Give the two most appropriate investigations.

The differential diagnosis clinically is between tuberculosis and CARCINOMA OF THE BRONCHUS. The radiological appearance of lobar collapse and a cavity is compatible with both. The assumption in this man was that his cavity was the source of his AAFB. However, in Europeans, tuberculosis affecting the anterior segment is extremely unusual. In fact, his carcinoma had broken down old healed tuberculosis in his right upper lobe, which was then recovered from his sputum. In some series, the recovery of dead tubercle bacilli from patients with a carcinoma of the bronchus is as high as 8%.

Culture of the sputum was sterile. The correct diagnosis would be reached by SPUTUM CYTOLOGY for malignant cells and after reporting of sterile sputum, BRONCHOSCOPY to confirm the diagnosis and assess operability should be performed.

Non-compliance was unlikely as the patient was under hospital supervision. The continuing malaise and fever could be explained by an adverse drug reaction, but as it was associated with radiological deterioration, this is very unlikely. In general, failure to respond to standard antituberculous chemotherapy could be due to infection with mycobacteria other than M. Tuberculosis. M. Kansasii can cause pulmonary cavitation and fibrosis. It is commoner among coal miners with pneumoconiosis and is probably not transmissible. The organism usually responds to standard antituberculous therapy, but other atypical mycobacteria, e.g. M. Avium, are often resistant to first line drugs.

Case 84

A 61-year-old printer presented with a month's history of abdominal distension and some weight loss. He mentioned his gait was funny; he felt as if his right leg flapped but he could feel the ground. He smoked 40 cigarettes a day, had a cough and some shortness of breath on exertion. He said he drank several pints of beer a day.

On examination he was thin and slightly jaundiced. He had several spider naevi and palmar erythema and a Dupuytren's contracture. There was ascites and a palpable liver 6 cm below the costal margin. Neurologically the only findings were a slight tremor and signs in his lower limbs. There was wasting of both calves together with some fasciculation. There was weakness of dorsiflexion and eversion of both feet, more marked on the right. The right ankle jerk was absent and the plantar responses were flexor. There was a slight reduction of sensation to touch and vibration in both legs.

Investigations showed Hb 12.4 g/dl (12.4 g%), MCV 110 fl (110 μ^3). Target cells in film. WBC 8 × 10^9/l (8000/mm^3). ESR 35 mm/h, bilirubin 113 μmol/l (6.6 mg%), alkaline phosphatase 210 U/l, aspartate transaminase 45 U/l, albumin 26 g/l (2.6 g%), α-foetoprotein – negative. Chest X-ray report: 'High diaphragms with some collapse at the left base – probably due to ascites'. Barium swallow, meal and enema normal. Liver scan – enlarged liver, patchy diffuse uptake of isotope. Liver biopsy – alcoholic cirrhosis with fatty changes. Lumbar spine X-rays normal.

1. What type of lesion, and at what site, would account for the motor symptoms in the right leg?
2. What are the four most likely causes of his neuropathy?
3. What would be the two most useful investigations at this stage?

This man has the classical signs of a lower motor neurone lesion, namely weakness and wasting of muscles with absent reflexes. The peronei and extensors of the foot are supplied by L4, L5 and S1 and hence these nerves must be affected somewhere along their course from anterior horn cell to muscle. The concomitant sensory changes suggest the lesion is a PERIPHERAL NEUROPATHY.

Other significant features in his history are his weight loss, heavy smoking and drinking, together with signs of cirrhosis and ascites. Of interest in his peripheral neuropathy is the preponderance of motor over sensory signs.

ALCOHOLIC NEUROPATHY must be considered but it is usually painful with marked hypersensitivity to light touch. Motor neuropathies are typical of PORPHYRIA or LEAD TOXICITY which might be relevant to his job as a printer. A motor neuropathy also occurs following infection (GUILLAIN-BARRÉ SYNDROME or, rarely now, with DIPHTHERIA) but there is nothing in the history to suggest this.

Taking into account the other features of the case, the most appropriate diagnosis would be CARCINOMATOUS NEUROPATHY, which typically gives both motor and sensory changes. In more than half the cases this is a non-metastatic complication of a bronchial carcinoma although sporadic cases occur with a variety of other malignant disease, including lymphoma. It may occur without any other suggestion of malignant disease and hence prompt and thorough investigation is necessary. We were temporarily distracted by the chest X-ray report but BRONCHOSCOPY and SPUTUM CYTOLOGY confirmed the presence of an oat cell carcinoma and laparoscopy visualised hepatic and peritoneal secondary deposits that were no doubt contributing to his ascites.

Diabetes mellitus and vitamin B12 deficiency both tend to produce a symmetrical sensory neuropathy and were rapidly excluded by biochemical tests. His macrocytosis was a manifestation of his high alcohol intake. There was no family history with this man to suggest any of the inherited causes of neuropathy.

Case 85

A 36-year-old engineer returned from Libya and went to see his GP with a three-month history of feeling unwell, weight loss, intermittent fever and shortness of breath on exertion for a year. He had also noticed that he had been passing large quantities of urine for six months and had had nocturia for the previous year. During the last three months he had become increasingly irritable and bad tempered and the quality of his work had deteriorated.

On examination he was clinically anaemic and had enlarged cervical glands. His cardiovascular system was normal. In his respiratory system he had expiratory rhonchi in the right mid and upper zones. His liver was palpable 5 cm below the right costal margin.

Investigations showed: Hb 7.5 g/dl (7.5 g%), WBC 9.0 × 10⁹/l (9000/mm³), ESR 40 mm/h, blood urea 38.0 mmol/l (230 mg%), blood sugar 5 mmol/l (90 mg%). Chest X-ray showed shadowing in right mid and upper zones and enlargement of lymph glands in both hilar areas. Plain X-ray of abdomen showed calcification of both kidneys which were of normal size. Sputum smears for acid fast bacilli were negative.

1. Give the most likely diagnosis and two other possibilities.
2. Give six important investigations to confirm your most likely diagnosis.

This man has nephrocalcinosis and is in renal failure. It is extremely likely that he has hypercalcaemia and this would explain the history of polyuria with progression to renal failure and his increasing irritability and poor work performance. His lung pathology may well be causing his hypercalcaemia and diseases which can give this radiological picture with hypercalcaemia include SARCOIDOSIS, RETICULOSES and CARCINOMA OF THE LUNG with or without metastases. Sarcoidosis is the most likely diagnosis in this case. Tuberculosis has been sought but it is very rare to see bilateral renal tuberculosis progressing to renal failure. Multiple myeloma with intercurrent infection could produce this picture and cause hypercalcaemia.

To confirm the diagnosis of sarcoidosis this patient should have SERUM and URINARY CALCIUM ESTIMATIONS and a KVEIM TEST. A LIVER OR CERVICAL GLAND BIOPSY would be helpful. A transbronchial lung biopsy might also be considered, and he should have X-RAYS OF THE HANDS to look for the changes of sarcoidosis and renal failure. PLASMA PROTEIN ELECTROPHORESIS is necessary. Levels of angiotensin converting enzyme may be raised in sarcoidosis.

Other diagnoses such as multiple myeloma or bronchial carcinoma would be excluded by normal bone marrow, absence of Bence-Jones protein in the urine, lung tomography and bronchoscopy and a skeletal survey for metastases or myeloma deposits.

Case 86

A 49-year-old cook went to see her doctor telling him that six days ago she had quite suddenly started to feel unwell with headaches, pains in her back and limbs, a dry cough, fever, malaise and a sore throat. Apart from painful ulcerating vesicles on her lips there were no other abnormal signs and she was advised to go to bed, drink plenty of fluids and take aspirin. Three days later the daughter asked the doctor to call and see her mother again as she had been breathless and more feverish for 24 hours, the headaches were worse and she preferred to be in a dark room. She smoked 15 cigarettes a day, drank occasionally and kept pet budgerigars. When examined the only abnormal findings were neck stiffness and a few scattered rales in both lung fields. On admission to hospital her lumbar puncture showed 2 cells, protein 0.4 g/l (40 mg%), glucose 3.3 mmol/l (60 mg%).

She did not respond to penicillin and her therapy was changed to oxytetracycline. She recovered slowly over the following two weeks.

1. Give three possible diagnoses.
2. What would be the five most useful investigations?

The normal CSF findings in this patient eliminate most of the commoner causes of meningism, mainly meningitis or subarachnoid haemorrhage. Meningism may occur as a reaction to fevers and is seen, for example, with influenzal and pneumococcal infections. The important features of this patient's illness are the mild respiratory and severe systemic symptoms, which suggest a viral infection, possibly complicated by a pneumonia (any debilitated person is likely to have an eruption of herpes simplex). The diagnosis of VIRAL PNEUMONIA is frequently missed on clinical examination by virtue of the paucity of physical signs in the chest. A CHEST X-RAY may reveal, as in this case, widespread patchy shadowing throughout both lung fields. Further clues to the viral aetiology of these pneumonias may be given by the absence of a neutrophil leukocytosis in the PERIPHERAL BLOOD and the failure to isolate pathogens on CULTURE OF BLOOD OR SPUTUM. The isolation of viruses from THROAT SWABS or the demonstration of RISING ANTIBODY TITRES may give a more accurate retrospective diagnosis.

MYCOPLASMA PNEUMONIA may be associated with the development of cold agglutinins in the sera and, as with other non-bacterial pneumonias, a false positive W.R. may be found.

LEGIONELLA PNEUMOPHILIA can cause a similar pneumonia with breathlessness, marked shadowing on the chest X-ray but usually a non-productive cough. Although the organism can be grown in special media, diagnosis is usually made serologically and treatment is with high dose erythromycin.

In view of the close association of this patient to birds, the possibility of an ORNITHOSIS must be considered as the clinical picture may strongly resemble any of the viral pneumonias. Finally, although influenzal pneumonia can occur alone, more commonly a secondary bacterial infection complicates the disease, of particular importance is a staphylococcal pneumonia.

Case 87

A 45-year-old bricklayer was admitted to hospital with a history of increasing dyspnoea over the previous four days. There was no history of chest pain, cough or haemoptysis. He had no previous illnesses and was on no medication. His mother had maturity onset diabetes.

On examination, he was not breathless at rest, but was slightly cyanosed. Blood pressure was 160/105 mmHg, radial pulse was 126 per minute and irregular, and of poor volume. His JVP was raised 2 cm and heart sounds were normal. In the chest there were fine inspiratory crepitations at both bases, and in the abdomen, the liver was palpable one finger's breadth below the costal margin. ECG showed atrial fibrillation with T wave inversion at leads V4−V6. Chest X-ray on admission showed cardiomegaly with LV prominence and pulmonary oedema.

The patient was treated with diuretics and oxygen. Cardioversion was unsuccessful, even using 400 joules. He was digitalised and on his other treatment his pulmonary oedema cleared, and his blood pressure settled to 140/90 mmHg. Serial chest X-rays showed gradual reduction in heart size.

Investigations showed: Hb 13.2 g/dl (13.2 g%), MCV 100 fl (100 μ^3), WBC 9.3 $\times$ 10^9/l (9300/mm^3), platelets 286 $\times$ 10^9/l (286 000/mm^3). Urea and electrolytes, glucose tolerance test and thyroid function tests were all normal. Viral titres showed no evidence of recent infection. Cholesterol 1.7 mmol/l (66 mg%) and triglycerides 10.6 mmol/l.

Echocardiography showed that the left atrium and both ventricles were enlarged. The mitral and aortic valves were normal. The left ventricle contracted poorly with an ejection fraction of 45%.

1. What is the likely diagnosis?

The patient has biventricular failure with atrial fibrillation. The ventricular rate is fast enough to tip a normal heart into failure. In this case, his atrial fibrillation is due to neither thyrotoxicosis nor mitral valve disease. There is nothing in the history to suggest ischaemic heart disease, nor a recent infection either viral or a bacterial pneumonia, both of which may precipitate atrial fibrillation.

There are several important pointers in this man's investigations, namely macrocytosis and a type IV hyperlipidaemia. The latter is commonly due to diabetes but the patient has a normal glucose tolerance test. These features, plus evidence on the echocardiogram, makes a diagnosis of ALCOHOLIC CARDIOMYOPATHY most likely. This condition often presents with arrhythmias, particularly atrial fibrillation. The findings of poorly contracting left ventricle and three chamber enlargement are not specific for alcohol, but indicate a congestive cardiomyopathy. Alcohol may affect the heart in several ways: apart from cobalt poisoning, and a congestive cardiomyopathy, the patient may develop thiamine deficiency (beri-beri) which clinically presents with high output cardiac failure.

Case 88

A 47-year-old male clerk presented with a long history of bronchitis and asthma. Failure to control the asthma with bronchodilators had necessitated the introduction of a small dose of steroids six months before admission. A month before he was admitted he had developed mild ankle oedema controlled initially by diuretics. Two weeks later he noticed increased swelling of his ankles, lethargy and generalised weakness. He had developed a cough productive of purulent sputum, and his wife said that he had become confused. He smoked 20 cigarettes a day and before admission was taking prednisone 5 mg daily, frusemide 20 mg daily, Slow K 1.2 g qds, salbutamol 4 mg qds and disodium cromoglycate capsules 1 qds.

On examination he was grossly cushingoid. He was ill but not confused and he was pyrexial (37.5). In the cardiovascular system his pulse was 100 per minute, regular rhythm, blood pressure 190/110 mmHg, JVP 3 cm elevated. Moderate ankle oedema was noted. The heart was clinically enlarged but no murmurs were audible. In the respiratory system widespread rhonchi were heard. In the abdomen the liver was enlarged to 3 cm below the right costal margin. Examination of the CNS revealed no abnormal signs except for generalised muscle weakness.

Investigations: Hb 13 g/dl (13 g%), WBC 6.9 × 10^9/l (6900/mm³), blood urea 6.5 mmol/l (39 mg%), plasma sodium 139 mmol/l (139 mEq/l), potassium 2.0 mmol/l (2.0 mEq/l), bicarbonate 24 mmol/l (24 mEq/l), chloride 94 mmol/l (94 mEq/l). Urinalysis showed a trace of protein, sugar + +, acetone negative. Chest X-ray showed consolidation of the lingula.

1. Give three causes for the recent development of his heart failure.
2. Give four possible causes for the development of weakness, lethargy and confusion.
3. A definitive diagnosis could be made by two investigations. What investigations are these?
4. Give 3 further relevant investigations.

Cardiac failure in this man may have developed as his long standing pulmonary disease with cor pulmonale may have been exacerbated by INFECTION, HYPERTENSION or FLUID RETENTION induced by his steroid medication.

His weakness, lethargy and confusion could be due to a combination of HYPOXIA, HYPOKALAEMIA and HYPERGLYCAEMIA. Both STEROID MEDICATION or an underlying MALIGNANCY could contribute to this clinical state.

The odd features in this case are the rapid development of a Cushingoid state on such a small dose of corticosteroids, and the occurrence of hypokalaemia despite large doses of potassium chloride. These findings in a heavy smoker with a shadow on chest X-ray suggest an ectopic ACTH secreting tumour of the lung. SPUTUM CYTOLOGY and BRONCHOSCOPY are mandatory (an oat cell tumour was found). His suspected Cushings Syndrome should be investigated by 24 hour free CORTISOL SECRETION and a DEXAMETHASONE SUPPRESSION test. Once Cushing's Syndrome has been established by non-suppression with dexamethasone, an ACTH LEVEL should be measured; this would be high in ectopic ACTH production, and on chromatography would probably be shown to be big ACTH.

Case 89

A 30-year-old school teacher presented with a history of increasing dyspnoea over the previous six days. For the past two years she had had 4 or 5 episodes of nocturnal cough, sputum and dyspnoea which usually followed an upper respiratory tract infection. These episodes resolved over a week with a course of antibiotics. Her only other problem was dysmenorrhoea for which she took the oral contraceptive pill. On this occasion she failed to respond and developed a sharp short-lived right lower chest pain.

On examination, her temperature was 37.5°C. She was not cyanosed and her blood pressure was 130/80 mmHg; pulse 100 beats per minute, sinus rhythm. In the chest there were bilateral expiratory and inspiratory rhonchi and a few crepitations at the right base, but no rub. The abdomen, legs and central nervous system were all normal.

Investigations showed: FBC – Hb 12.8 g/dl (12.8 g%), WBC 9.6 × 10⁹/l (9600 mm³). Sputum culture was sterile. ESR was 25 mm/h. Chest X-ray showed some soft shadowing at the right base.

Her penicillin was changed to tetracycline and she was given bronchodilator tablets. A week later she felt considerably better and, although she continued to expectorate a little mucoid sputum, she was well enough to return to work. However, one month later she had a further episode of dyspnoea and on this occasion had coughed up a few flecks of blood mixed with some sputum.

On examination she was slightly breathless with evidence of mild bronchospasm. There were no other abnormal physical signs.

Chest X-ray showed resolution of the right lower zone changes, but newer shadowing at the left apex with the suggestion of some ring shadows was noted. ECG was normal. A ventilation/perfusion lung scan showed no evidence of pulmonary emboli.

1. What is the diagnosis?
2. Give three helpful investigations.

The patient gives a history of episodic dyspnoea often precipitated by upper respiratory tract infection. The physical findings are predominantly those of bronchospasm and in a previously fit, non-smoking patient, bronchial asthma is by far the most likely cause. This, however, has been complicated by an abnormal chest X-ray. The most common cause is bacterial infection and although sputum culture was sterile, the patient had had several days treatment with antibiotics. She does, however, develop some new X-ray changes and has a small haemoptysis. While this obviously raises the possibility of pulmonary emboli, this is unlikely without a perfusion defect with normal ventilation on lung scanning.

The appearance of transient pulmonary shadowing in an asthmatic is very suggestive of ALLERGIC BRONCHOPULMONARY ASPERGILLOSIS. This is characteristically associated with BLOOD and SPUTUM eosinophilia and a POSITIVE TYPE 1 PRICK TEST TO AN EXTRACT OF ASPERGILLUS FUMIGATUS. Serum precipitins are less consistently present and culture of Aspergillus from the sputum is not universal. The concentration of immunoglobulin E (IgE) in the serum is usually raised but is non-specific.

Proximal bronchiectasis may occur at the site of previous infiltration and may explain the haemoptysis in this patient.

The disease is a potentially serious complication of extrinsic asthma and has been reported in as many as 20% of asthmatics admitted to hospital. It is a hypersensitivity reaction to Aspergillus fumigatus affecting bronchial walls and peripheral parts of the lung. The airway obstruction is often more than usually severe and there is a moderate reduction in gas transfer factor. Transient infiltration leaves permanent radiological change in half the patients and often leads to permanent functional impairment with bronchiectasis and lobar shrinkage. The diagnosis is important to make early as treatment with corticosteroids diminishes the frequency of acute attacks and reduces the likelihood of severe permanent lung damage.

Case 90

A 38-year-old barman presented with a two day history of headache. This had been preceded by a short illness with myalgia, malaise and anorexia. Three years previously he had been hospitalised with an unexplained attack of abdominal pain, but which had settled after 36 hours of conservative treatment and had not recurred. He smoked 20 cigarettes a day and drank at least 4 pints of beer every night. His general practitioner had started him on Penicillin three days prior to his admission.

On examination, his temperature was 38°C, blood pressure 130/76 mmHg, pulse 92 per minute and regular. Examination of the heart, chest and abdomen was normal. Examination of the central nervous system revealed mild neck stiffness and a positive Kernig's sign.

Investigations: Hb 12.9 g/dl (12.9 g%), WBC 9 × 10⁹/l (9000/mm³), ESR 45 mm/h, blood sugar 6.4 mmol/l (115 mg%). Urea and electrolytes, liver function tests and chest X-ray were all normal. Lumbar puncture showed 400 white cells per cubic millimetre (70% lymphocytes, 30% neutrophils). CSF protein – 1.5 g/l (150 mg%), sugar 2.4 mmol/l (43 mg%), gram and ZN stains of CSF showed no organisms. Culture of CSF was sterile.

In addition to his penicillin, chloramphenicol and sulphadiazine were added to his treatment. The patient remained febrile and unwell. Five days after admission he became drowsy and confused. His neck stiffness and headache worsened and neurological examination showed bilateral brisk reflexes, extensor plantars and impaired upward gaze.

1. What is the most likely diagnosis?
2. What would be the immediate management?

The patient has aseptic meningitis which could be due to partially treated bacterial meningitis. The predominance of lymphocytes in the CSF, however, raises the possibility of a viral or tuberculous aetiology, or, more unusually, a fungal or malignant cause. The combination of a lymphocytic pleocytosis and a low CSF sugar should be assumed to be due to TUBERCULOUS MENINGITIS until proven otherwise. The absence of stainable organisms on direct microscopy does not invalidate the diagnosis, nor would a normal chest X-ray which is present in 25% of patients with tuberculous meningitis. Treatment should begin at once with TRIPLE THERAPY: RIFAMPICIN, ISONIAZID and STREPTOMYCIN. The value of intrathecal antibiotics is still debated.

Subsequent events are suggestive of raised intracranial pressure and mid-brain distortion. In this context, the development of a COMMUNICATING HYDROCEPHALUS is the most likely diagnosis because of impaired resorption of CSF due to damage to the arachnoid granulations by meningitis.

Immediate management includes a CT BRAIN SCAN to look for dilated ventricles and possible peri-ventricular lucencies (implying a recent acute rise of intracranial pressure). It will also help to exclude a cerebral abscess, especially if contrast medium is given. Management includes high dose DEXAMETHASONE and transfer to a neurosurgical centre for consideration of ventricular drainage. The CSF must be examined again in a further attempt to isolate mycobacteria and exclude other possible causes of aseptic meningitis. The CSF should be examined for malignant cells and fungal and bacterial infections excluded with Indian ink and gram staining respectively. A viral meningoencephalitis could cause a similar clinical picture and CSF and serum should be sent for viral studies to exclude this retrospectively. The diagnosis of partially treated pyogenic meningitis is often very difficult, but serology may again be helpful. Sarcoidosis and collagen diseases may both cause meningeal involvement, but both are rare and clinical and other laboratory evidence is necessary in making these diagnoses.

Case 91

A 78-year-old lady was admitted for investigation. For the past two months she had been generally unwell, lethargic and anorectic and complaining of generalised muscular pains and arthralgia in shoulders, hips and wrists. Her general practitioner had tried her on an iron/folate combination after vitamin tablets had not improved her symptoms. On the week before admission she had become slightly confused at night with a tendency to fall.

Past medical history included a cholecystectomy 30 years ago and a myocardial infarction six years previously, from which she had made a good recovery. She had been on bendrofluazide 10 mg daily since her myocardial infarction.

On examination she was well orientated, with a temperature of 37.3°C. Her conjunctivae were pale with two small petechiae on the left. She was not cyanosed or dyspnoeic. Her blood pressure was 160/95 mmHg; pulse 100 beats per minute and regular with a fair volume. The left ventricle was enlarged. The heart sounds were normal with a soft pansystolic murmur at the apex. Her respiratory system was normal, and in the abdomen the spleen tip was just palpable. The central nervous system was normal, with no proximal muscle weakness. General examination showed osteoarthritis of the left knee and Heberden nodes on the fingers. Both temporal arteries were palpable and non-tender.

Investigations showed: Hb 9.8 g/dl (9.8 g%), MCV 86 fl (86 μ^3), MCH 1.8 fmol (29 pg), MCHC 19 mmol/l (30 g/dl), WBC 8.6 × 10⁹/l (8600/mm³), platelets 470 × 10⁹/l (470 000/mm³), ESR 78 mm/h. Urea and electrolytes and liver function tests were normal. Chest X-ray showed left apical calcification and moderate cardiomegaly. Serum B12 and red cell folate were normal. Serum iron was 10 μ/l (56 μmol/g%). Total iron binding capacity was 36 μmol/l (201 μg%). MSSU showed four red cells/high powered field, with no growth.

1. What is the diagnosis?
2. How would you confirm the diagnosis and give six other useful investigations.

This patient demonstrates the non-specific presentation of illness in the elderly. She is anaemic with splenomegaly, red cells in the urine and a vasculitic lesion on the left conjunctiva. In addition, she has the murmur of mitral incompetence and this is strongly suggestive of INFECTIVE ENDOCARDITIS. The elderly often present with little or no fever and with a long non-specific history. Several other diagnoses should be considered, e.g. polymyalgia rheumatica, tuberculosis and disseminated malignancy. In this case, a renal tumour is a possibility and INTRAVENOUS UROGRAPHY and URINE CYTOLOGY should be performed.

The anaemia is that of chronic disorder. A myeloproliferative disorder could present in this way and a BLOOD FILM may reveal immature cells. BONE MARROW EXAMINATION may show stem cell replacement with tumour, myeloma or fibrosis. This should also be CULTURED for tubercle bacilli and CULTURE of SPUTUM for M. TUBERCULOSIS performed. The diagnosis is made by BLOOD CULTURES, the most common organisms being Staphylococcus epidermidis or Streptococcus viridans. The haematuria in subacute bacterial endocarditis is multifactorial, but is usually due to immune complex glomerulonephritis and is suggested by a C_3 hypocomplementaemia in the serum.

Case 92

A 34-year-old woman presented at the dermatology outpatients after urgent referral from her GP. She had a widespread rash affecting her mucous membranes, arms, palms of her hands and soles of her feet which had started one day previously. Before the rash occurred she had been feeling unwell for several days and had been started on antibiotics for a respiratory tract infection five days before. She had not been abroad and had no history of contact with anyone with a similar disease.

On examination she was ill, pyrexial (38.5°C) and had erythematous macules in different stages of evolution on her palms, arms, soles of her feet and orogenital mucosa. She also had injected eyes and small ulcers on her conjunctivae. Some of the skin lesions had a central blister.

1. What is this condition and give three possible aetiologies?
2. What four investigations would you perform?

This is a typical case of quite severe ERYTHEMA MULTIFORMAE or Stevens-Johnson syndrome and she has some lesions with a central blister, typical of the target lesions seen in this condition. The underlying aetiology of this condition is frequently not found, but here a DRUG SENSITIVITY rash is most likely. These are commonly associated with sulphonamides and penicillin antibiotics, which she may well have had. Other important causes of erythema multiformae include STREPTOCOCCAL INFECTIONS and VIRAL INFECTIONS such as herpes simplex. Other diagnoses are much less likely. However, with lesions on the palms and soles of the feet, SECONDARY SYPHILIS, the great mimicker, must be considered. With orogenital ulceration and bullous lesions such diseases such as pemphigus and pemphigoid should be considered, though she is young for these and pemphigus has a more protracted course. Pemphigoid and another possibility, bullous dermatitis herpetiformis, are more chronic and have less mucous membrane involvement and fewer systemic symptoms. She does not have any of the other features seen in Beçhet's syndrome. This is unlike chickenpox (polymorphic rash) and the only other possibilities would include septicaemia or systemic lupus erythematosus, or rarely a lymphoma.

Investigation must be aimed initially at finding an aetiological agent. As the lesion is produced by an immune complex, the antigen should be sought looking for streptococci by THROAT SWABS and BLOOD CULTURE, and an ASOT and sequential VIRAL STUDIES should be performed. SEROLOGICAL TESTS FOR SYPHILIS should also be done. SECONDARY INFECTION should be sought by culturing lesions and collecting blood cultures. If there is any doubt about the diagnosis, SKIN BIOPSY will confirm the diagnosis and exclude rarer diagnoses such as pemphigus, pemphigoid, dermatitis herpetiformis and lymphomas.

Case 93

A 63-year-old woman presented with a two month history of polydipsia, polyuria, weakness and lethargy. Further questioning elicited a short history of a dry cough of some three weeks' duration, angina on effort, anorexia and recent weight loss.

On examination she was ill, febrile and dehydrated with a fine tremor. The pulse was 84 per minute in regular rhythm, blood pressure 150/75 mm Hg. There was no cardiac failure. Expiratory rhonchi were audible in the chest, but there were no other abnormalities.

Preliminary investigations showed: Hb 9.4 g/dl (9.4 g%); WBC 13 × 10⁹/l (13 000/mm³) (90% polymorphs), ESR 111 mm/h, Plasma sodium 151 mmol/l (151 mEq/l), potassium 3.5 mmol/l (3.5 mEq/l), chloride 107 mmol/l (107 mEq/l), bicarbonate 27 mmol/l (27 mEq/l). Blood urea 3.3 mmol/l (20 mg%), blood sugar 6.9 mmol/l (125 mg%), bilirubin 6.8 mol/l (0.4 mg%), alkaline phosphatase 182 U/l, total protein 69 g/l (6.9 g%), albumin 28 g/l (2.8 g%), serum calcium 2.9 rising to 3.1 mmol/l (11.6 to 12.2 mg%), phosphate 1.0 falling to 0.87 mmol/l (3.1 to 2.7 mg%). Urine microscopy showed red blood cells greater than 30 per high power field, white blood cells 2. The culture was sterile.

1. What is the most likely diagnosis?
2. Give two other possible diagnoses.
3. What six further investigations would you initiate?

Hypercalcaemia is a recognised cause of polyuria, polydipsia and dehydration. Prolonged hypercalcaemia causes tubular damage with impairment of urinary concentration and can give rise to renal failure with nephrocalcinosis. In this patient there is no evidence of severely impaired glomerular function (blood urea 3.2 mmol/l, 20 mg%). However, the finding of haematuria raises the possibility of pathology in the urinary tract and in view of other features in this patient, a RENAL CARCINOMA should be considered a possibility. The hypercalcaemia could be due to parathormone secretion by a renal carcinoma, PRIMARY HYPERPARATHYROIDISM or to METASTATIC CARCINOMATOUS involvement of bone though other conditions such as milk alkali syndrome and sarcoidosis should also be considered.

A careful evaluation of her fluid balance state is indicated and PLASMA and URINE OSMOLALITIES estimated. In this case, a raised serum osmolality (310 mosm/kg) was associated with a low urine osmolality (110 mosm/kg), showing impairment of tubular concentration. HYPERCALCURIA was also present.

Investigation for the underlying cause of the hypercalcaemia should include a CHEST X-RAY and INTRAVENOUS PYELOGRAM. In this patient cannon-ball secondary deposits were obvious on the chest X-ray and distortion of the calyces on intravenous pyelography suggested a primary renal tumour. A SKELETAL SURVEY or BONE SCAN may show evidence of bone destruction if the hypercalcaemia is due to metastatic carcinoma. SPUTUM and URINE CYTOLOGY would be indicated in this patient and may give a histological diagnosis. The measurement of PARATHORMONE by radioimmunoassay may show a raised level in primary hyperparathyroidism or inappropriate parathormone secretion.

Case 94

A 37-year-old Welsh woman gave a history of progressive onset of breathlessness over a three month period. Apart from a dry cough there were no other symptoms, and she had previously been in good health. Six months before admission she had had a hysterectomy for fibroids.

On examination her general condition was good. Early clubbing was noted and dyspnoea was evident on the slightest exertion, together with central cyanosis. Apart from a prominent pulmonary second sound, examination of the heart was normal. However, fine crepitations were audible in the mid and lower zones on auscultation of the chest. Examination of the alimentary and central nervous systems revealed no abnormalities.

Investigations: Hb 14.0 g/dl (14 g%), WBC 6.0 × 10⁹/l (6000/mm³), ESR 12 mm/h. Chest X-ray showed a fine linear pattern most evident in the lower zones. Arterial gases: PaO₂ 7.7 kPa (58 mmHg), PaCO₂ 5.1 kPa (38 mmHg), pH 7.41.

1. Suggest two possible causes for this patient's presentation.
2. What two further investigations would you perform for each diagnosis?
3. What immediate treatment would you give?

The history of cough and progressive breathlessness in the absence of any clinically demonstrable cardiac disease suggests a primary pulmonary cause for the symptoms. Left ventricular failure due to any cause, for example congenital or rheumatic heart disease would be unlikely in the absence of cardiomegaly. The previous history of a pelvic operation raises the possibility of MULTIPLE PULMONARY EMBOLI and should be considered (chest pain and haemoptysis are not invariable accompaniments of this condition). This presentation is, however, classical of FIBROSING ALVEOLITIS. The findings of clubbing, cyanosis and fine (crackling) crepitations in the lung fields are characteristics, as are the X-ray changes. Other forms of pulmonary fibrosis such as sarcoid or lymphangitis carcinomatosa may present in this way.

Sputum examination for malignant cells should be performed. However, the essential investigations in this case would be tests of LUNG FUNCTION such as FEV_1, FVC, measurement of transfer factor, lung compliance and repetition of arterial blood gases before and after oxygen administration. An ECG should be performed. If emboli are suspected, PHLEBOGRAPHY, LUNG SCANNING and perhaps right heart catheterisation with PULMONARY ANGIOGRAPHY would be indicated. The further investigation of pulmonary fibrosis necessitates testing for possible extrinsic allergens, for example, skin tests, avian precipitins. A Kveim test for sarcoid and measurement of rheumatoid factor, ANF and DNA binding might suggest other causes for her fibrosis. In certain cases lung biopsy may be indicated.

The treatment of cor pulmonale includes DIURETICS and DIGITALIS, although the latter is of doubtful efficacy in this situation. 100% OXYGEN in this situation may be given. In extrinsic allergic alveolitis, steroids are indicated. With multiple pulmonary emboli even at this late stage ANTICOAGULANTS must be given.

Case 95

A 44-year-old woman went to her GP because she had lost a stone in weight over six months and during this time she had intermittent epigastric pain. Two weeks previously she had developed a generalised itchiness and had noticed that her urine was dark coloured. She had never been in hospital before, she drank only a small amount of alcohol and had not been in contact with anybody with jaundice. She had not taken any medications nor had she been given any injections in the past 6 months.

On examination she was jaundiced and had rubbery nodules on her elbows. Other physical signs were confined to her abdomen where she had an enlarged smooth liver palpable 10 cm below the costal margin, no ascites and no splenomegaly.

Investigations: Hb 12.0 g/dl (12 g%), WBC 8.0 × 10⁹/l (8000/mm³), bilirubin 85.5 μmol/l (5 mg%), alkaline phosphatase 280 U/l, aspartate transaminase 30 U/l, serum cholesterol 9.3 mmol/l (360 mg%), chest X-ray normal.

1. Give four possible causes for her disease.
2. Give four causes for her disease.
3. What six investigations would you perform?

This middle-aged woman has a six-month history of illness leading to an obstructive jaundice. The important differential diagnoses to consider include GALL STONES, PRIMARY BILIARY CIRRHOSIS, SECONDARY DEPOSITS probably from a primary tumour of the gastrointestinal tract, or a TUMOUR IN THE HEAD OF THE PANCREAS compressing the common bile duct. As her serum transaminase is not markedly raised, this makes the diagnoses of progressive cirrhosis or hepatitis less likely, though it does not rule them out. Her intermittent epigastric pain may be due to CHOLELITHIASIS, RECURRENT CHOLECYSTITIS, possibly PEPTIC ULCERATION or even PANCREATITIS associated with carcinoma of the pancreas or gall stone disease.

Investigations must delineate if there is obstruction to her biliary tract. A LIVER SCAN may be helpful in that it could show multiple space-occupying lesions. An ULTRA-SOUND will show dilated bile ducts if there is a distal block to the biliary tract. BARIUM STUDIES would delineate gastrointestinal pathology and show an intestinal neoplasm, though pancreatic carcinoma may not always be diagnosed on barium studies. If biliary obstruction is diagnosed on an ultra-sound, an ENDOSCOPIC RETROGRADE CANNULATION OF THE COMMON BILE DUCT should be attempted to locate the block. MITOCHONDRIAL ANTIBODIES are found in 95% of patients with primary biliary cirrhosis and a LIVER BIOPSY may well be indicated after assessing bleeding and clotting function, though the dangers of biliary peritonitis should be considered. If the diagnosis is not revealed by these investigations, a diagnostic LAPAROTOMY should be carried out.

Case 96

A 22-year-old Turkish man, studying history at the local university, presented to Casualty complaining of lower left pleuritic chest pain. This had started suddenly that morning and gradually worsened. There had been no associated cough or haemoptysis. In addition, he had noticed some tenderness of his right lower leg.

He was normally well, although he had had to drop out of the university hockey team on two occasions during the previous winter due to pain and swelling in firstly his left knee and then his right ankle. The team doctor had evidently attributed these to trauma during preceding games.

He was on no regular medication but took an occasional aspirin for headaches, smoked 5–10 cigarettes per day and did not drink. One month earlier he had returned from visiting his mother in Turkey; his father having died of 'fluid overload' in his early thirties.

On examination, he was febrile with a temperature of 39.2 and had obvious severe pleuritic chest pain with rapid shallow respirations. There was some local chest wall tenderness over the area of pain and breath sounds were diminished. A pleural rub could not be heard. On the skin of his right leg below the knee was a hot tender swollen erythematous area approximately 4 × 7 cm.

Investigations in Casualty showed: Hb 14.4 g/dl (14.4 g%), WBC 12 × 10^9/l (12 000/mm^3) (N = 70%, L = 26%, M = 2%, E = 2%), ESR 50 mm/h. Urea and electrolytes normal. ECG – sinus tachycardia but otherwise normal. CXR showed a small left pleural effusion. Urinalysis: protein + + + +, blood negative, glucose negative. Urine microscopy revealed no cells or organisms.

1. What is the diagnosis?
2. What is the likely outcome of the acute attack?
3. What is the long-term prognosis?
4. How would you treat the condition?

This man presents with the typical features of FAMILIAL MEDITERRANEAN FEVER. This is an inherited disease occurring in populations originating on the South and East coasts of the Mediterranean and usually seen elsewhere in Sephardic Jews.

The disease consists of repeated attacks of fever and painful serositis manifest usually as synovitis, abdominal pain or pleurisy. In some cases, the attacks are associated with an erysipelas-like skin lesion on the lower leg, as in this man. Attacks occur unpredictably and are of sudden onset with fever as a prominent early symptom. Pain and fever generally begin to abate after a few hours and recovery is usually complete in 48 hours although joint effusions may take much longer to resolve, and may occasionally be chronic.

A proportion of patients with familial Mediterranean fever develop amyloidosis and proteinuria can occur either before or at a variable time after the other features of the disease. Renal failure secondary to amyloidosis used to be the usual mode of death, but patients are now treated with dialysis and transplantation.

An effective therapy for the febrile episodes has now been found with patients taking regular COLCHICINE which both reduces the frequency and severity of the attacks. Once an attack is established there is little to be done beyond providing pain relief. There is hope that colchicine therapy may hinder the development of amyloidosis.

Despite the typical features other causes for this man's symptoms must be considered. A primary lobar pneumonia is not uncommon in this age group and may initially have no radiological signs. A pleural effusion however would be unlikely without evidence of consolidation. Tuberculosis is a distinct possibility in those from the middle-east but is unlikely to present so acutely. A pulmonary embolism would not cause so high a fever. Systemic lupus erythematosus could cause many of the features but is rare in young men and attacks as acute as this one would be uncommon. Polyarteritis nodosa is unlikely to cause such pronounced proteinuria and the joint symptoms.

Case 97

A 36-year-old Spanish waitress was admitted three days after returning from Madrid, with severe colicky central abdominal pain, radiating to the back. When admitted she passed one loose stool. Her periods were regular. There was no significant past medical history and she was on no medication.

On examination, her temperature was 38.5°C and she was sweating profusely. Her pulse was 120 per minute, regular; blood pressure 160/110 mmHg. There was generalised abdominal tenderness, but no guarding. Rectal examination was normal, and there was no blood or mucus in the stool. Examination of the heart, chest and central nervous system was normal.

Investigations: Hb 12.8 g/dl (12.8 g%), WBC 11.0 × 10⁹/l (11 000/mm³), reticulocytes 1%. Sodium 138 mmol/l (138 mEq/l), potassium 3.4 mmol/l (34 mEq/l), urea 3.8 mmol/l (23 mg%). The aspartate transaminase was raised at 48 U/l, but the serum albumin, alkaline phosphatase and bilirubin were normal. Serum amylase was 240 U/l. Stool culture grew no pathogens. Midstream specimen of urine was sterile and contained no cells. Plain abdominal X-ray and chest X-ray were normal. Ward testing of urine (Dipstick) showed urobilinogen ++, but no bile.

The patient was thought to have cholecystitis, but despite treatment with nasogastric suction, intravenous fluids, analgesia and broadspectrum antibiotics, her condition failed to improve. Over the next 72 hours, her fever continued and she developed increasing abdominal pain.

At laparotomy, the small bowel was rather dilated, but there was no evidence of intestinal obstruction. The gall bladder contained a single small stone, but there was no evidence of acute inflammation. Cholecystectomy was performed and a normal appendix removed. Post-operatively she had further abdominal pain, persistent tachycardia and a prolonged paralytic ileus. She remained febrile. Four days post-operatively her blood pressure dropped from 105/60 mmHg, to 70/40 mmHg, pulse 140 per minute, regular. A chest X-ray was normal and ECG showed a sinus tachycardia. She was thought to have a gram negative septicaemia and was treated with penicillin, gentamicin and metronidazole, as well as intravenous fluids, plasma expanders and hydrocortisone.

Examination of the laparotomy scar showed no evidence of a collection or discharge through the wound. Her intra-abdominal drains showed only a little serous fluid. Her Hb was 12.3 g/dl (12.3 g%), WBC 13.0 × 10⁹/l (13 000/mm³). Sodium 132 mmol/l (132 mEq/l), potassium 3.6 mmol/l (3.6 mEq/l), urea 4.2 mmol/l (25 mg%). Blood sugar 6.3 mmol/l (113 mg%). Blood cultures were sterile on four occasions. A CT scan of the abdomen with contrast enhancement showed no evidence of an intra-abdominal abscess.

1. What is the diagnosis?
2. How would you confirm it?

This lady presented with severe abdominal pain, but no evidence of peritonitis. Following an essentially negative laparotomy, the pain worsened, was associated with a prolonged paralytic ileus and persistent hypotension. Despite adequate treatment of a presumed septicaemia, she remained unwell. Other causes of post-operative deterioration, such as myocardial infarction and massive pulmonary embolus were excluded. An intra-abdominal abscess was excluded by CT scanning and peri-operative perforation of a viscus was clinically unlikely. It is in these circumstances that ACUTE INTERMITTENT PORPHYRIA should be considered: the severity of the abdominal pain with an incongruous paucity of physical signs, deterioration following an anaesthetic (barbiturates), and labile blood pressure are all features of this condition. A further pointer was the presence of a normal serum bilirubin and the absence of haemolysis in the presence of a positive reaction of the urine to Ehrlich's reagent. Both porphobilinogen and urobilinogen give a red colour when mixed with Ehrlich's reagent. However, if with the addition of n-butanol the red colour does not enter the upper butanol layer, it is porphobilinogen (Watson-Schwartz reaction). The diagnosis rests on the demonstration of increased URINARY 5-AMINOLAEVULINATE (ALA) AND PORPHOBILINOGEN which are the hallmark of an acute attack. Occasionally, the diagnosis is made after the urine has been noticed to darken on standing due to oxidation of porphobilinogen to porphobilin.

Management of the condition is complicated by the exacerbation of symptoms by a wide range of drugs. Neurological involvement with inadequate respiration and bulbar symptoms may be fatal and require long periods of intermittent pressure ventilation. The disease is inherited as a Mendelian dominant and the rest of the patient's family must be screened.

Case 98

A 16-year-old cashier presented to Casualty with a two week history of swelling of her ankles. Shortly before the onset of this, she said that she had had an upper respiratory tract infection and sore throat but had recovered uneventfully. She was otherwise well, smoked 20 cigarettes per day and drank an occasional Babycham. She was on no medication.

In her past history she had suffered from the usual childhood diseases and had had her appendix removed two years previously. Her father was a diabetic controlled on insulin and there was no family history of renal disease.

On examination, she looked well, but had rather sunken cheeks. Her mother stated that she had had a normal round face until shortly after an attack of measles at the age of six years. Her blood pressure was 145/80 mmHg and her venous pressure not raised. She had pitting oedema of both ankles to mid-thigh level. Routine urinalysis showed $+++$ protein and a moderate amount of blood.

Investigations initially showed: Hb 11.7 g/dl (11.7 g%), WBC 11.2 × 10⁹/l (11 200/mm³), ESR 50 mm/h. Her electrolytes were normal and a blood urea 4.0 mmol/l (24 mg%), with serum creatinine 120μ mol/l (1.4 mg%). Total plasma protein 50 g/l (5.0 g%), with albumin 18 g/l (1.8 g%). Fasting glucose 5.0 mmol/l (90 mg%). Anti-nuclear factor negative. IVP normal. 24 hour urine protein 12 g.

1. What is the diagnosis?
2. What complement abnormality would you expect to find?
3. What is the treatment and prognosis?

This girl presents with oedema, hypoproteinaemia and heavy proteinuria, all characteristic of the NEPHROTIC SYNDROME. In addition, she has the characteristic facies of PARTIAL LIPODYSTROPHY. In this condition, there is symmetrical loss of fat from the face with or without disappearance of fat from the arms, chest, abdomen and hips, but with normal distribution on the lower extremities. The aetiology is unknown, but an infective illness is often present at the onset. It is commoner in females and usually presents between 5–15 years of age.

Roughly a quarter to one third of patients with partial lipodystrophy have a clinical nephritis and a much larger proportion have complement abnormalities. The characteristic renal lesion is MESANGIOCAPILLARY GLOMERULO-NEPHRITIS where histology shows moderately hypercellular glomeruli with thickened capillary loops. This is due to both mesangial cell interposition and to deposited immunoglobulins.

The complement abnormality found is a LOW SERUM C3 CONCENTRATION but with normal levels of the earlier complement components of the classical pathway, CIq, C4 and C2. This suggests that C3 is activated via the alternative pathway and a factor – the C3 nephritic factor – has been found in the serum of these patients which acts in this way.

The course of mesangiocapillary glomerulo-nephritis is one of continuing disease and slow decline into renal failure and there is no good evidence that steroids or immuno-suppressives modify the course.

Symptomatic treatment of the nephrotic syndrome with diuretics may be necessary and supporting stockings are often helpful. Hypertension and urinary tract infections should be watched for and treated. When renal failure intervenes, she will require treatment with dialysis and possible transplantation.

Case 99

A 50-year-old woman was admitted as an emergency. She had been under the care of the haematologists for two years with chronic myeloid leukaemia, treated with intermittent courses of busulphan and prednisone.

Her leukaemia had been discovered after a routine blood count prior to her hysterectomy for fibroids. She smoked 20 cigarettes per day.

Ten days after her last course of chemotherapy, she developed a dry unproductive cough. Two days later, she had become dyspnoeic and this had worsened despite ampicillin from her own doctor.

On examination, her temperature was 38°C and she was profoundly cyanosed. Her respiration was 34 per minute, pulse 120 per minute and regular. Her heart sounds were normal and venous pressure was not raised. Examination of the chest was normal. The liver and spleen were enlarged 2 cm.

Investigations: Hb 11.3 g/dl (11.3 g%), WBC 30 × 10^9/l (30 000/mm^3), platelets 186 × 10^9/l (186 000/mm^3). Urea and electrolytes and liver function tests were normal. ECG showed sinus tachycardia and partial right bundle branch block. Chest X-ray showed bilateral soft basal and midzone shadowing of a reticular pattern. Blood gases – pH 7.50, PaO$_2$ 6.1 kPa (46 mmHg), PaCO$_2$ 3.5 kPa (26 mmHg).

1. What is the most likely diagnosis?
2. How would you establish it and what other investigations would you do?

This patient presents the common clinical problem of an immunosuppressed patient with an acute intercurrent illness. In this case, there is a characteristic syndrome of cyanosis, tachypnoea, a clinically clear chest and widespread radiological shadowing. This is most suggestive of PNEUMOCYSTIS CARINII pneumonia. A bacterial pneumonia is possible, but one would expect more focal signs, a productive cough, and some response to broad spectrum antibiotics. Busulphan therapy not infrequently causes pulmonary fibrosis and functional impairment, but does not present so acutely. Pulmonary embolism may present with dry cough and dyspnoea, but despite the previous pelvic surgery is most unlikely in this situation and the ECG findings are non-specific.

Diagnosis depends upon demonstration of the organism. Sputum culture is positive only rarely and BRONCHOSCOPIC WASHINGS and BIOPSY give a higher yield. LUNG BIOPSY, however, may be required as it allows silver staining of a sizeable piece of lung tissue.

Candida and aspergillus can cause a similar picture, but in the case of the former, there is usually evidence of candida elsewhere, and aspergillus pneumonia is usually focal. Both organisms may be cultured from the sputum. Viral pneumonias (e.g. Herpes, Mycoplasma) can be diagnosed on rising titres of viral antibody. BLOOD, THROAT and URINE CULTURE are of course necessary to exclude infection in these sites – and in fact even in immunosuppressed patients, 90% of infections are bacterial.

Pentamidine therapy has the advantage of specificity for protozoal organisms and consequently has some diagnostic value when the infective agent has not been isolated. However, treatment may cause unpleasant systemic reactions, abnormal liver function tests and nephrotoxicity. COTRIMOXAZOLE is now more commonly used given as 14 tablets per day or an equivalent intravenous dose.

Case 100

A 46-year-old Irishman presented in Casualty complaining of the sudden onset of left loin pain radiating to his left groin. He stated that he had had similar previous attacks of pain, usually left sided but occasionally on the right. He had been told he suffered from renal stones and had been hospitalised several times in Ireland, the last time six months previously. In his past history he had also had an operation for an ulcer and operations for adhesions, all in Ireland. He was a labourer, unmarried and had come to England three months ago. He lived in a bedsit and denied any drugs or medications.

On examination he was writhing in agony and was afebrile. Abdominal examination showed four laparotomy scars and he was slightly tender in the left loin. There were what appeared to be venepuncture marks on the right arm.

Initial investigations gave Hb 14.5 g/dl (14.5 g%), WBC 7.4 × 10⁹/l (7400/mm³), ESR 4 mm/h, urea and electrolytes normal. Chest X-ray and abdominal X-ray were both normal. Urinalysis – blood + +.

A diagnosis of left renal colic was made, he was given a dose of pethidine and admitted under the urologists where a subsequent MSU was sterile and an IVP was normal. Daily urinalysis confirmed persistent haematuria.

He complained of no further loin pain but two days later developed tight central chest pain radiating to the left arm. On examination, he was not sweating or dyspnoeic, but seemed in severe pain. Pulse 72/minute and regular, blood pressure 110/70 mmHg, venous pressure not raised, heart sounds normal, chest clinically clear. He was given diamorphine and transferred to the coronary unit and kept under bedrest and close observation. His CXR was repeated and was unchanged and serial ECGs showed an old inferior myocardial infarction but did not change. His cardiac enzymes did not become raised and whilst on the coronary unit his haematuria was noted to have disappeared.

1. What is the diagnosis?
2. What is the treatment and prognosis?

This man gives two classical clinical histories, firstly of renal colic, and secondly of ischaemic heart disease, neither of which is substantiated on investigation. In addition, his past medical history is made difficult to confirm, he has multiple laparotomy scars and has possibly had a recent hospital admission, as evidenced by venepuncture marks. All these make it likely that he is suffering from MUNCHAUSEN'S SYNDROME. In addition, his haematuria, readily faked when on a general ward, disappeared when he was kept under close observation.

Munchausen's syndrome is applied to patients who have made hospital admission a way of life. They often present with dramatic symptoms and can go to elaborate lengths to feign their disease; many with chest pain often have abnormal ECGs, as with this man. The symptomatology is often wide and when one group of symptoms is in danger of being discovered a fake, they may change to a second group. They often have evidence of multiple previous operations, usually laparotomy scars or burr holes. The past medical history they give may be elaborate and is usually extremely difficult to substantiate. This problem is increased by the fact that they often use differing names at their admissions.

The syndrome is named after a fanciful character of fiction, Baron Munchausen, who was himself based on an 18th century Hanoverian army officer of the same name. Both these characters were renowned for exaggerated and extraordinary stories.

Most Munchausen patients take their own discharge as soon as discovery is imminent. Hence, evaluation of the psychopathology is difficult, let alone the fact that they are known to be individuals who deliberately lie to mislead. It is seldom justifiable to detain such patients compulsively and with their elusive nature no treatment can usually be offered. This is perhaps just as well as no effective treatment is known and failure has been reported with hypnosis, ECT and leucotomy. The patient's elusiveness makes long-term outcome uncertain.

Their multiple hospital admissions distinguish them from simple MALINGERERS and the short non-continuing nature of this man's pain together with the absence of any withdrawal symptoms, make it unlikely that he is a DRUG ADDICT wanting more of his drug.

If possible, it is helpful to obtain a photograph of the patient for any subsequent identification.